T0090523

ASCENSION 101

a spiritual workbook and read

PSYCHA SUPERNOVA

BALBOA.PRESS
A DIVISION OF HAY HOUSE

Balboa Press books may be ordered through booksellers or by contacting:

Balboa Press
A Division of Hay House
1663 Liberty Drive
Bloomington, IN 47403
www.balboapress.com
844-682-1282

Because of the dynamic nature of the Internet, any web addresses or links contained in this book may have changed since publication and may no longer be valid. The views expressed in this work are solely those of the author and do not necessarily reflect the views of the publisher, and the publisher hereby disclaims any responsibility for them.

The author of this book does not dispense medical advice or prescribe the use of any technique as a form of treatment for physical, emotional, or medical problems without the advice of a physician, either directly or indirectly. The intent of the author is only to offer information of a general nature to help you in your quest for emotional and spiritual well-being. In the event you use any of the information in this book for yourself, which is your constitutional right, the author and the publisher assume no responsibility for your actions.

Print information available on the last page.

ISBN: 979-8-7652-4705-1 (sc)
ISBN: 979-8-7652-4704-4 (e)

Balboa Press rev. date: 11/14/2023

TABLE OF CONTENTS

***Disclaimer: this book contains spiritual content which
may lead you to ascension.**

DEDICATIONS

Let me explain, that any famous names from history that I mention are simply past life regression explanations, and each god or goddess is split between 5 souls in my personal opinion. For instance, say you have the Buddha. Well his soul reincarnates with multiple souls/guardian angels and is split in one past life. This means when there is reincarnation, his soul is split again between multiple people or spirits. This is the explanation why someone would have a bestfriend/ twin soul. It is likely you are very close to your bestfriend because you shared a lifetime together in the past, and you are still connected so the Universe brought you together again. This book is dedicated to my spirit guides and my star family. Katrin/Grandma/Sailor Moon/Jezebel/Lakshmi/ Beset- my guardian angel twin soul that steals my heart and I will always love forever. Thank you for saving my life, multiple times. Travis/Grandpa/Greenman/Osiris/Bes/God thank you for being my best friend in times of need and having beautiful energy that is unbreakable.

Shakti/Liz/Kali/Queen Elizabeth-thank you for your headstrong energy when you know I need it. I love you and I am grateful for your divine feminine crazy ass energy. Shiva/Zach/Atlas/Archangel Zadkiel/Telegonus-I know you understand me and I love you! Thank you for having my back and your sweet sarcasm.Saint Lisa B/Berkano Goddess-I love you thank you for being on my side and with me during the hardest times.Lisa/Faerie Goddess thank you for your playful energy I love you.Helen of Troy/Grandma C I appreciate you and I love you so much! Thank you for being there for me. Paris/Grandpa C I love you and I love that our stubborn asses can make jokes lol.Vince/Angel of Light/Lucifer-keep saving the world you are appreciated we love you.Aunt Gwen with the blue eyeshadow you are funny love you. Rosalee your wisdom is appreciated.Odin Banana my fierce dragon of fire you are a lovable beast that is special to this earth.Lobo I miss you.*Welcome home sweet Jakey/Jackie O, I love you.*Iyengar you are an inspiration to my yogic practice.Kuan Yin thank you for being a teacher in self love.Emily Thorne thank you for your dance moves,Tom Who for helping me have sweet dreams,Sasha Bonasin for your light readings,Sef Alchemist for helping me find my Daemon journey, Sri and Kira beautiful souls I love you,Joni Patry thank you for your astrology lessons. Kurt Cobain,Amy Winehouse,Juice World,Jesus Christ/ Grandpa, Mother Earth/Grandma I admire you. Pentangle the band thank you for speaking to my heart.My brother Chris/King Henry the 8th/Hanuman/Aeetes has loved me unconditionally and accepted me 100% my whole life, I have always appreciated that mutual connection. *Let's keep going up.* Monica/Raven helped me find spirituality in a time of my life where I was open and ready, I hope this book will help someone else do the same one day. I am forever grateful to know my guides.To my birth father *Helios* thank you Dad for teaching me to never stop gaining knowledge, and that I can accomplish anything with my life. Thank you to my mom (mermaid nymph goddess) and stepdad (christian viking) for supporting me through some heavy moments of my life and sticking by my side. Persephone and

Perses (Stephaney and Justin) I love you and I only want the best for you both. I love all of my family and I do hope they can look past any nonsense and accept who I am. I am Kat/Psyche/Freya/Isis. I love my soul and spirit, I am here to help this planet and show you your shadow. I will love you forever and my spirit is shaking.Also this is dedicated to all the souls that I have crossed paths with and I hope you find your way on this unique journey we call life.I love my *soul family* and only wish that they will also find *Ascension 101* useful. One way to figure out your past lives is to think about how your name is spelled and what letters stick out,and realize that resonating with a story or image is probably not just a coincidence, it's because you have been here on earth before. It is likely whoever you have encountered in this lifetime are a part of your soul family. If your soul resonates with someone from history, take that very seriously. *Blessed Be *

others worth mentioning that I want to thank for being sweet that I wish an amazing journey and know that you are in my prayers/thoughts; Shere, Marian and Deb, Naomi, Paisley and Everly, My moms side of the family, Garrett and Carolyn, Katie, Nick, Lexie, Athena,Serena,Val, Torre and Maria, April, Aston and Bentley,Astrid the Yoga teacher, Jason Towne Artist, Alex from Refuge Recovery,Kamala,Hilary Safe Haven and Aspen,Joelle, Therece, Auntie Mel, Rima, Yuli, Both Melindas,Jasmine, Jeana, Tabitha, Crysta, The Best Virginia and Larry, Sam the body worker, Kenzie- Pot Pie Til I Die, Bill TieDye, Jesse the Psychic, Strawberry, Akasha, Ty, Alex, Norman, Justin, Sandra, Cousin Bradley, Liz and Sam, Kristi, My dad's side of the family, Jennifer soul mom, Jake and Carlton, Jessica, Krissy, Tiffani and Sarah with the cats, Katie the yoga teacher, Nicole O., Sabrina the Psychic, Amine I am happy for you, Chris H., Kat from the coast, Rachel and Chris, Tomcat, Sitara I love you, Milly and her Nana and Papa, Cherry, Megan and Greg, Shushan, Tara and Noah, Kimmy, Cindy, Lisa, Kim, Nada and Zeh, Amber, Jenna Unitarian Church, Kristi C., Michael, Gage, Reagan, Jenn, Jenn and Dakota, Helena, Brett and Jessica, Denise and Charlie, Dominay, Charlene, Bethany, Amy, Taylor, Michael, AJ, Sarah, Gabby, Jared, Tyler H., Tyler Sp., both Christians, Daniel, Caitlyn and Caleb, Kenny and Jake, Clayton and Connor, Dylan, Dylan T., Maddy, Breanna, Jackson, Teagan, Chris, John, Cody, Josh, Gaylen, Cody G, Joey, Joey K, Gianna and Hannah, Lacey, Kat, Kacey, Ron, Krystal, Sarah, Sam, Sammi, Sam, Joaquin, Emmy and Christine, Scarlet, Charlie, Edith, Jaime, Nolan, Omar, Ryan Drummer, Eva And Dave, David Eddy, Tim, Steve, New Frontiers and Whole Foods, Clint, Carl, Keith, Andrea, Annie H, Lucas, Austin, Corey, Sunrisa, George, Paul, Gina, Isaiah, Rainy, Lupe, Sharon, Ish and Adrian Karenia and Maria, Lori Granger, Seymour, Teddy, Patricia P., Marina G, Sheri and Barry, Nick, Crystal, Margaret Namasta, Tomas and Shelley (I dream of a spiritual connection like that), Raul Recording Artist, Tim Unitarian, MDr. Atwhal, Dr.Guimaraes, Dr. Amen, Dr. Abiola, Stacey counselor, Susan Counselor, Stacey sponsor, Barclay, Leslie sponsor, and Frigg. R.I.P Scotty, Corey, Vince, Travis, Liz, Zach, Wolfgang, TOM AA, Lisa, Wendy cousin, the grandparents and Brody. Thank you to the Ecstatic Dance community in San Luis Obispo, Santa Barbara, and Fresno for amazing high energy experiences. Thank you to Touchstone Recovery and Herndon Recovery. Thank you Ann the psychic, Robert the psychic, James the psychic, Sylvie, and Terry Yoder.

Thank you to The Open Eye, The Brass Unicorn, The Crystal Barn, Earth's Virtue, Ziayas's, Artifacts, Paradise Found, and The Mystic Merchant (metaphysical shops in California) for being sweet. Thank you to Joanne and Giovanni and the yoga studios in California including Harmony House, Old Town Yoga, Manifest Station Yoga, Sol Seek Yoga, Four Corners for a spiritual sweat. Check out Sycamore Hot Springs, Mono Hot Springs, and Esalen for the most relaxing experience you can find. Fun Music Festivals you should go to: Lucidity, High Sierra, SnowGlobe, Tomorrowland, Electric Forest, EDC, Burning Man, Lightening in a Bottle, Coachella, Bhakti Fest and Shakti Fest, Joshua Tree Music Festival, RiSE Festival, Aftershock, Firefly, California Roots Festival, and be safe! Stay tuned imma make my own freaking Hogwarts!!! Thank you to all my massage clients, and anyone I forgot to mention, I LOVE YOU ALL!!!! Thank you Asmodel. <3 speak with your soul…

PERSONAL NOTE

Louise Hay, the queen of affirmations, had a positive and vibrant attitude, and was inspiring to many. Listening to her helped me on my journey. She was a real saint and goddess with her outlook and ability to help so many people. I'm also a huge fan of Dr. Wayne Dyer, another HayHouse author who is now with us in spirit. I came across a CD set at this metaphysical shop of the audiobook "Wishes Fulfilled: Mastering the Art of Manifesting"- by Dr. Wayne Dyer. Well one day I was listening to the tapes, and then my soul sista told me Dr. Wayne Dyer had crossed over recently. I felt really connected to his spirit, like he may have known that somewhere on earth, someone and probably many others were listening to his voice, his words of positive wisdom; while his soul was leaving the planet. He had a sweet soul and kind heart, just listening to his voice will always be soothing to me. Thank you Hay House and Balboa Press.

My guides and soul family are leading my path; only to be closer to my universal lessons. Thank you karma, and thank you like-minded souls who can say Ascension 101 helped them on their spiritual journey. Find your soul purpose and mission in life.

PREFACE

I was struggling in 2013 after experiencing a drug-induced psychosis. I went to a hypnotherapist/ psychotherapist in the town that I grew up in- and ended up clicking with her. She used a pendulum to clear my chakras while she hypnotized me with meditative techniques. I grew up learning to read tarot cards from my grandmother and going to metaphysical shops, but hadn't been introduced to pendulum work until then. Monica told me that I could ask my angelic team/ my spirit guides questions, and they would give me a yes or no answer. I have helped people start talking to their own guides and shown them how simple it is to use a pendulum. When she told me angels were with me I *believed* her. I started asking the angels questions related to the afterlife. This led to me finding my connection to the higher power that I now call the Spirit of the Universe. "Talking to the angels" literally has changed my whole life. I ask them simple things, complicated things, pretty much anytime I have a question about anything that I know I can't answer myself. I even ask them- can you help me find my pendulum? They help me so much, and now they give me direct messages (for me it's clairaudient mostly) all the time as my number one cheerleaders for spirit. Questioning life triggered the shenanigans of my spiritual awakening. My soul is happy for divine intervention, and this book is meant to help you find *yours*.

"The mindful cactus is a wonderful place, but you need to live in the real world. And in the real world, cake happens."

"I am Less interested in your higher power, more interested in your inner power." Script from the T.V show Mom (Season 5, Episode 14)

Mom is produced by Chuck Lorre Productions in association with Warner Bros Television.

These quotes are from the character Miranda, a spiritual energy cleanser, who has a session with another character at an A.A retreat in the show. Miranda starts performing the energy cleansing and starts singing to Christy (main character) who is lying on the table. Miranda starts making weird noises during an abrupt energy removal. It gives you a playful way of looking at energy work, and I couldn't take my eyes off the screen.It's a hilarious episode. This just reminds me of how I met my hypnotherapist, and how "energy work" changed my life. When I was under hypnotism and meditation, my chakras were opened. I learned how to communicate with my angels. I had so many questions for my guides about my life and the world, like is my guardian angel with me all the time? That answer is yes. Spirituality has changed my life. It has made me a better person and more open minded.

READY TO ASCEND AND KEEP THAT VIBE UP???

All that hype about being WOKE is real.

Divine feminine is an energy to embrace. Until we are equal there will be no peace/silence. People have masculine and feminine energies in them. Not to be f**ked with. - Kali Ma (channeled message from spirit)

Mediumship, the cycle of the moons, plants from the ground, tattoos, cursing, women, and being gay are now widely accepted. *Lucifer* is a god of self worth. His gift is to shine light on addictions, chaotic influence, and bring confidence to decision making.

I want to live where soul meets body
And let the sun wrap its arms around me
And bathe my skin in water cool and cleansing
And feel, feel what it's like to be new
Song -Soul Meets Body- Death Cab for Cutie

Ascension 101 is a mini spiritual guidebook, for everyone who is interested in creating harmonious energy, and coexisting with others in peace. A book for empaths and people who want to *grow* and *change* as a person. It's about loving yourself and loving life. Ascension 101 has meditations and exercises, and includes info about forms of divination, crystals, frequency, manifestation, healthy foods, yoga, and how to take care of your environment. We are in a multiverse of existence and are able to connect to the heavenly realms if we are open. Awaken the higher self and let limitations and insecurities become something of the past. *Kiss my Bliss.*

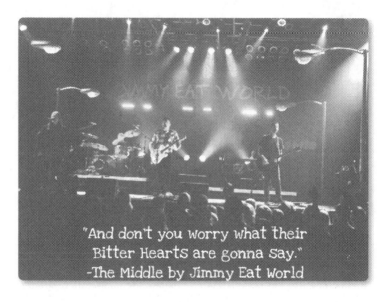

"And don't you worry what their Bitter Hearts are gonna say."
-The Middle by Jimmy Eat World

Affirmation: *I AM LIVING MY LIFE FOR THE HIGHEST GOOD, THANK YOU UNIVERSE FOR ALIGNING MY ENERGY WITH THE BEST VERSION OF MYSELF. I AM ALIGNED WITH THE MOST HIGH FREQUENCY VIBRATIONS AND LOVE*

*say it and believe it in your heart chakra

If you don't believe in faeries- take a look around the garden. Life is short.

There is no doubt that getting "woke" has helped people find their spiritual awakenings across the globe. As a side note, this has been a long time coming prediction for the "Age of Aquarius". For you to kiss my bliss and tell others to do the same; you will need to find self love. Loving yourself looks different for everyone. Simply put, hocus pocus and abracadabra are just the tip of the iceberg. In this guidebook we will go over positive affirmations and green smoothies, so take what you need. You don't have to wear a mud mask to practice self care but coincidentally we will be sharing recipes for great skincare. Self love is an art that is mastered differently by every human, it is not a competition or race. It is truly loving yourself (unconditionally) enough to want to keep living on this planet with the rest of us minions. The routines and practice you choose are entirely what fits you and your life. The self love domino effect is global for good reason.

BACK TO LOVING YOU

In America, The Self-Love Movement in the 1950s was created by the Beat Generation, which were the hippies before Woodstock. After World War II, societies started promoting "peace and love", which that british band, The Beatles, pretty much endorsed. Spirituality became more popular than ever, which is obviously happening AGAIN (so cool huh). Self-Love rituals are more than lavender eye pillows, staying sober for the weekend, doing a juice detox,going to the gym on a Saturday night, getting your hair done, or taking a selfie. It's accepting your insecurities and embracing fear. It's having a true, authentic relationship with ourselves. *Treat yourself. Treat yourself nice.* This revolution of equal rights, acknowledgement of past traumas, and embracing your inner child is really starting a movement lately. A spiritual movement. An evolution of healing, creating peace. Everyone has different opinions, and the more we respect each other's values, boundaries, and light-hearted point of view, the more peace we will create. There are monks that go years without even speaking, and no one is harassing them about it. In fact they have widely accepted quotes that are more inspiring than some political leaders.

Creating positive affirmations and self talk is something pretty common now. Turn negativity, denial, and self esteem issues into acceptance, love, and freedom. Appreciate the bones in your body and life on earth because YOLO (you only live once). Self-care is popular for sure, pretty soon enlightenment will be even more popular (at least hopefully anyways). You may have already heard some ancient but more recently popular spiritual activities in modern society: (drum roll) YOGA, holding rocks, reading about plants, wearing jewelry as protection from the evil eye, using herbs, creating magick spells, or using essential oils (spooky right?). How about compassion anyone ever heard of that blasphemy? LOL JK. I welcome all beings of light into this personal space of acceptance, equality, peace, and judgment-free zone as you read Ascension 101.

You are loved. You are Beautiful. You are inspiring. When you do healthy things, your soul gets good vibes, and your spirit guides are clapping in joy. Your soul is electric. It is on fire, and made up of all the elements. Everything is a big freaking test. Think about things in your life lately. Why have they happened or what led up to them? Who else on earth is going to take credit for what you have done with your life? *You* get to take credit for everything. Whether it be a big mistake, or your greatest accomplishment in life. These things are your responsibility, and this is your reality right now. Are you in a happy place? Are you struggling? Be in the moment. Just be alright. You're reading this book. Maybe you will get something out of it.

Meditate.

Pause.
Breathe.
Eat a salad.
Squash a bug.
Slay.

. . . .

Lol i'm just kidding, don't squash a bug that's mean.

Throughout *Ascension 101*, you will find Questions I created for beautiful, willing, random, awesome people to answer. **A handful of individuals have openly shared their perspective. Hopefully you will enjoy the heartfelt, genuine answers scattered in the book. You will get the vibe from these different people. It's been an eye-opening, wonderful experience for me to get to know them.**

One more thing… I poured my heart and soul into this book. I wish to be with my soul family once again, in outer space.

Pain is Love
Suffering is Earth
Peace and joy is ..
our reward
Rebirth is beautiful

We Love You

CHAPTER 111

CRYSTAL VISIONS/CLEARING ENERGY/ CHAKRAS/CREATING INTENTIONS

The angel number 111 means your dreams are being manifested; and you are attracting wealth.

Energy Cleansing/ Energy Work

So, it's good to be aware that our bodies can pick up on energy. Vibrations in your chakras create subtle tingly sensations that make you feel bad or good. Fear, attachment, and insecurities can cause a cycle of negative feelings. Butterflies in your stomach, overwhelming guilt, excitement, pleasure, anger, all these take on a form in the body and can stay with us for periods of time. **You need to protect yourself as a spiritual being.** Icky energy can be avoided and released.

CLEARING happens when negative energies leave your body. It's important to release whatever no longer serves you, *give your guides permission to cleanse your spirit*, or find a **method** yourself. This is why spiritual practitioners are hired to clear the energy of a home with sage. You can tell the energy of a home or your body using your *intuition*. To *heal* and clear all negativity from the physical and the multidimensional realms around you, it would be advisable to practice some form of energy work. ***Reiki*** is an ancient

Buddhist practice that can be very healing for your soul/ body. This involves certain hand placements on yourself or another person.

"My intentions are Clarity, Peace, and Serenity, I will Bless you with my love in my Reiki Practice."

If you believe in *spirit guides*, or a *higher power*, you can ask aloud or in your mind to place a *shield of protection* around your *auric field* or someone else's. It helps if you **believe**

that they can help. *Thank them* and acknowledge *them* for helping you.

My guides, please keep me safe and protected today. Thank you for guiding my path for the highest good. I love you, please protect me. Archangel Michael please protect my space and energy, thank you blessed be.

Meditation takes practice, focus, and skill to master. Visualization is a perfect method for clearing unwanted energy and creating **light**.

Mini Visualizer

Put both feet on the ground and feel the connection to the earth. Close your eyes, imagine white light radiating from your heart, getting bigger and bigger. Keep focusing, breathing and creating a big beautiful bright white light with your mind's eye until it's as big as the room, filling up the whole city you live in. Imagine the whole world/ universe with rays of white light washing the streets, oceans, jungles and so on. There is a silver cord of white light grounding you to the earth as your bright light is shining. Open your eyes and have a beautiful day, staying connected and protected.

Cleansing Your Energy Methods

- Sprinkle **salt** in between doorways and window sills for protection from harmful spirits or entities/bad energy - replace every so often

- Create a **circle of salt** around you for protection (or before spells)
- Place salt around your bed frame for protection- you can also draw salt in a pentagram or another protection symbol or sigil
- Epsom salt baths will clear energy, quick and easy solution for empaths exposed to narcissistic abuse
- Use a Lemon or Lime body **spray**

(Create your own with vodka and essential oils) spritz away creating **good vibes! (Florida Water)**

- **Send reiki energy** anywhere in the world to those in need of healing/protection/love
- Ask **Archangel Michael** to cut ties with people that are toxic and ask Archangel Rapheal for healing energy-(perhaps if a person has cancer or any health condition,emotional trauma)
- **Smudging** with **sage** -Native American tradition that is used in spiritual ceremonies to cleanse, purify and pray. *Clear* the energy in your body, clear the space of your home, or use as a tool to clear *objects* of negative energy
- A Scottish folk magic practice called "**saining**", cleanses negative spirits on people, places, objects, and livestock. The meaning of sain roots from seun- a charm- that blesses or makes the sign of the cross (celtic)- protecting your prosperity and to hollow and awaken.
- **Palo Santo-** Shamanic stick that removes negativity and obstacles and attracts good fortune

- **Sweetgrass**- used by the Woodland Indians, believing it is Mother Earth's hair representing mind, body and soul.

Many different cultures kept these sacred plants alive-with knowledge- to pass down to generations to come- there is much to appreciate that the earth gives. Wave these sacred herbs over your body under the arms and around the head or even better have someone with good energy do it for you.

- **Quartz** is for clearing energetic space while welcoming angels and guides
- **Selenite** is for clearing the energetic debris of other stones/crystals and raising the vibration- the stick can be waved around your body for protection
- To clear your crystals, place them in a bowl of **salt for 24 hours** or into the earth for 24 hours and they will be cleared by the moon and charged by the sun. You can also place them on your window sill for the same effect.
- Ask your guides to clear **energy of a crystal w**hile holding it- then leave it alone somewhere safe
- Ask your guides to **clear your chakras-** ask politely for an energetic cleanse (right before bed is great)
- **Ask your guides** for protection and clarity

Example : "Energy which no longer serves me- releases into love and light -I ask that all unwanted energy is swept up into the clouds. Thank you angels for assisting this energy into the light. I only attract energy with positive intent and am in servicework on earth. Anything negative is transmuted into the heavenly realms. I am grateful for this process."

- Use pendulum to clear away any negative on an object or yourself
- When you feel a negative feeling from a negative being say **"release now"**
- **Chant** OM, chant Hindu/Hare Krishna mantras, sing to clear vibrations to attract a sound of peace
- Sing sea shanties/Viking music/Pagan witch songs
- Music @ Love Frequency 528 hz or high vibration
- **Mantras**- positive affirmations
- **Hymns**-songs of worship/honoring gods/saints/goddess
- **Black tourmaline** is for protection
- **Obsidian** is for Transmuting negativity
- **Pyrite**(transmutation)
- **Meditation** can cleanse your mind and spirit
- Connect to your **higher self**
- Shakers like a **spirit stick** (make one yourself like I did)
- **Reiki** which involves hand placements to heal the body's energy frequency and chakras
- **Pranic Energy Healing** which involves physically removing energy blockages with your hands out of an area of the body which is affected, placing it into a bowl of salt that is flushed so that energy is removed, it's removing the energy from your body. Visualize a waterfall/body of water/the wind/the stars/a healing energy sweeping away (use your imagination) to release that negative energy
- Energy clearing with a pendulum over each chakra
- **Body scanning** meditations
- **Tapping** which helps the nervous system to regulate
- Asking for spirit to help you *transmute* the energy and speaking out loud *I AM A POWERFUL TRANSMUTER*

- *Sprinkle **Eggshells** with intention for protection
- Remove hex/curse with egg cleansing (slowly rub/move the egg along body until you feel like it is in the egg, drop into water to see if someone is sending you bad vibes, then flush it with chili powder and tell them they are **exposed**)
- Any harmful entities that you *sense, tell them you command them to leave and they are exposed and caught up by all the guides and we know what you are trying to do, you have to leave now because you are exposed. Any spirit that has ONLY benevolent intentions is welcome to stay. All other energies are exposed, be gone.*
- ***SHAKE YOUR BODY/DANCE it out***
- ***Kundalini yoga***
- ***Boundaries with people***
- **Acknowledge all spirit encounters and address them right away**

Why should you protect yourself from energies that are not helpful? Because when your energy is cleansed, you are fully functioning at a high vibe. You'll be in touch with your highest self, let go of everything unwanted or not needed on your soul journey. The progress you make is personal and in divine timing. Release old ways of thinking, creating new healthy habits and paying attention to your growth. Be your own #1 fan. Be confident about energy cleansing, you have the power to let things go.

How to Sage yourself or others..(Kats way)

Ask your guides to protect your energy, ask that all negative energies are released and set free. Use an abalone shell to hold the sage/palo santo so you don't get ashes everywhere. You can do it inside or outside. ***Remember you can clear***

your energy anytime of day, anywhere using any method.
Take your arms out wide, I like to do a circle of smoking sage
around my head, on top of the arms, under the armpits, I get
my ears alot (they are super sensitive to energy since I'm more
clairaudient), both sides of the legs, circle around the head
again, get the back side. Of course your backside is easier to get
when you have a friend to do it for you. Same thing when you
are doing it for someone else. I like to close with circling my
head and doing a cross in front of my head and around the ears
again. SOMETIMES YOU WILL NEED TO USE MORE,
SOMETIMES LESS. It depends on what exactly is happening
with the vibes. Over time you'll understand what that means.

How to make a shaker for clearing energy..

(My idea came from the show Orange is the New Black when the character Lolly carries a spirit stick every morning and uses it to protect herself/ her energy)

You'll need:

- A stick of some sort

(I used a Halloween solar lamp garden stick with an eyeball that flashes)

- Bells or anything that makes noise that you can attach
- Any art work you want to add

I wrapped blue yarn around the whole thing and attached Christmas jingle bells. You can do anything you want, make it your own.

Your unique spirit stick can be used in the car, your home, anywhere you feel you need it. I use mine just like sage, it's really powerful. Shake it all around yourself, clearing your energy around your body and your environment. In a pinch, you can even use your car keys or anything that rattles. Whatever you use, it's your unique energy and your shifting that vibe quickly.

Have fun :)

Oh yeah you can shake your body too! That's a **very** quick method to release any stagnant energy- that also involves Kundalini energy but we will get into that later ;).

House Blessing/Affirmation

If you are living in a house, say a positive affirmation before you walk in or when you leave."My home is protected." or "This house is protected by angelic beings of light." "Guardians watch this house." Affirmations work when you are confident with what you say. Raise the vibration of your aura, your home, those around you, and the world.

Example: "I am safe.""I am that I am. I am love. I am light. I am at peace. I am protected by my spirit guides/angelic team and I am worthy and accept myself. I emanate light, love and justice. Any negative entities or debris of any sort may leave now. This environment is safe, protected, and of holy light. This space is clear. Angels guard this space."

Setting a Morning Routine/Ritual

Questions ***

Does positivity help your daily routine?

Starting off the day with meditation, self reflection, and positivity sets the foundation so you are ready to attack what the day brings. I do intentional movement when I wake up.

-Mike Gilbert

Writing out your plans for the next day before bed is a great way to set yourself up for success. Your morning ritual could include yoga, essential oils, avocado toast, dancing, yerba mate, mindfulness. Make the morning count and start off the day with positivity so you can keep that going throughout the day. Accomplish a few small things on your list so you feel like you did something. Give yourself credit and live your best life!!

Crystal Visions

"I keep my visions to myself."- Stevie Nicks

On a high note, the infamous glittering rocks that amaze the average tarot reader; **crystals**.

Crystals are widely wanted and hold a special energy. Just like we all carry "vibes" around with us; so do crystals and even other objects. You may wonder, these powerful stones are beautiful, but what do I do with them? Besides being pretty to look at and having different spiritual meanings, they hold energy. So if you touch a crystal with good vibes or bad, that energy will latch on to the crystal. They hold energy similarly like an animal, plant, or human. This is why they are sensitive and should be cleared often. Moonlight, sunlight, and salt will do the job. When a crystal is cleared, any negative energy can go up into the heavenly realms and disperse. That is why it is important to ask your guides to clear energy off of other objects. Think of it as if you had just rolled in the mud and you wash off the mud with a hose; same concept. This is also what happens with your chakras. Selenite (the salt stone) clears all crystals. You can wave your selenite stick around other crystals saying something like - "this selenite removes all negative debris and entities or dark energy stuck on my crystal. Higher vibrations circulate new energy that transforms all negative to the highest good." You could even put a circle of salt around your crystals with intention.

Mini list of my favorite crystals to vibe with….

Amethyst - **promotes sobriety and clarity, calmness, protection, Pisces vibes**

Rose quartz- **romantic love, unconditional self-love, compassion, heals emotional wounds, Taurus vibes**

Clear quartz- **Angelic communication, clarity, cleansing, positivity**

Obsidian- **Transmutes negative vibes, grounding, blocks psychic attack sagittarius vibes, cuts away negative energy**

<u>Shungite:</u> creates protective force shield

<u>Tigers eye</u> : grounding, setting boundaries

<u>Turquoise</u>- creativity, good fortune, wisdom, luck, tranquility, protection, enduring love, sagittarius vibes

<u>Jade</u> - stone of good luck, serenity, purity, friendship, harmony, attract wealth, aquarius vibes

<u>Citrine</u>- attract abundance, health, wealth, success, scorpio vibes

<u>Labradorite</u>- magick stone, heals chakras, protects the aura, transforming energy, finding courage within

<u>Lapis lazuli-</u> truth stone, spiritual enlightenment, self expression, creativity, sagittarius vibes

<u>Selenite</u>- clears all crystals and chakras, brings high vibration quickly, angelic healing, taurus vibes

<u>Green calcite</u>- heart chakra opener

<u>Pyrite</u>- Transmuter, protection against bad energy and psychic attacks

<u>Howlite</u>- Virgo Stone, artistic expression, channeling anger into something better,

<u>Rainbow Moonstone-</u> clairvoyance, intuition

Black Tourmaline- absorbs negative energy, shield against toxicity, purity, helps with decision making, Libra vibes

Malachite- associated with heart chakra, prosperity, luck, capricorn vibes

Celestite - angel stone, reflective and meditative, universal guide, infinite wisdom, compassion

Spirit Quartz- harmony, alignment, and nurturing spiritual growth.

Azurite- clears throat chakra, intuition, harmony in the heart, clear decision making, strength

SPIRITUAL WARRIOR

Relationship with your rocks

Talk to crystals just like you would talk to a house plant or animal. You can pray to them and ask for that message to be sent to the source of everything, or even find comfort in knowing the energy they hold and what you FEEL when you hold them. Lay on your bed with a crystal on your forehead and receive the energy that it has had for many millions of years, and absorb it. Wire wrap them if you feel drawn to that type of hobby/work. Create a *crystal grid* which helps to align your intentions. Mediate with them, sleep with them in your hands for protection, keep them in your bra, or lay on the ground with a bunch of crystals surrounding you. Put them on your body in each chakra placement to see how that feels for you.

"You say you got a vision, take my hand and tell me what you see
You can read between the lines cause your my palm reader
Got your crystals in your pocket like a drug dealer
Now you're telling my future
No, and I believe ya
You know I gotta have it
Feels like black magic"
Palm Reader- By DREAMERS, BIG Boi, UPSAHL

The Chakras

Muladhara- Red-(1st)-Root Chakra- this is the chakra that makes you feel grounded to the earth. Centered and secure. Stability. Red jasper, dark stones like obsidian, shungite, tigers eye, and even incense like dragon's blood can help you to feel connected.

Svadhisthana- orange- *Sacral* -2nd chakra- sexual drive, connected to the moon and waters, carnelian, sunstone

Manipura- Yellow-3rd chakras- solar plexus- belly button, self esteem and confidence, having control over your life, citrine

Anahata-Green- 4th chakra-heart- open your heart chakra with green calcite, this is where your love is affected for yourself and for others, so keep it open by saying i love you and protect your aura with kind words that are meaningful and true- rose quartz, jade

Vishuddha-Blue-5th chakra-throat - where your voice truly comes from, chakra blockage creates fear in voice/ communications, keep your blue throat chakra open and lifted with blue kyanite, sodalite, lapis lazuli- (truth stone) *my voice is powerful i love the sound of my voice*

Ajna- purple- 6th chakra-Third eye- the pineal gland- the chakra giving insight and knowledge of your true self, seeking guidance, especially important decisions. Freedom of thought.

Sahasrara- Violet or White-7th chakra- Crown- in Sanskrit translates to "thousand petals" Violet flame- above the head- encompassing your whole aura/spirit. Affirmation: *I am that I am.*

Chakra meditation.

Record yourself saying this reading and then listen quietly in a setting without distraction.

Imagine a dresser drawer with 7 drawers. Now imagine each drawer is a different color, the colors of all of the chakras. The root drawer is a deep red, grounding you to the earth, keeping your balance, and everything under control. Your sacral is a bright orange, keeping your sex drive and hunger in balance. Your solar plexus keeps your body centered, a sunny color of yellow that keeps a consistent happy mood. Next is your heart drawer, all your green desires and abundant love that you have for people open up, glowing for the world. "My heart is open. I am an empathetic human that resonates with loving others. I have time to hold the space when other people need me. I am seen as a caring individual." Then we get to open the throat chakra drawer, which is blue and cool. It brings you awareness how people love to hear you speak and that your words are important. You are heard. "My words are so powerful. I use the best intentions when speaking to people. They listen to me and I listen clearly. My voice is gleaming with clarity when I sing and speak loud and clear. Your third eye is purple, it is right in between your eyes and holds the space for creative spiritual thoughts, for divine emotion and connection with higher vibrations. "I am a divine human. I am loved, understood, and use self expression. I am a highly intuitive human being." Your violet starr above that is gleaming with purple into white and you are connected to the heavenly realms and holy spirit where you live in acceptance of yourself and others. You now experience balance in all colors and energy drawers and feel enlightenment on all levels. I am that I am. I am that I am. I am that I am.

I invoke the violet flame and live in the highest light.

OPEN YOUR CHAKRAS PRACTICE AND MEDITATION

Sometimes, people can feel a little bit toxic on your path or journey in life; and as an empath your energy is vulnerable at times.

You will need:

An image of the 7 chakra colors on your phone/computer, something with rainbow colors, something that changes colors, or draw the colors of the rainbow on paper.

Light a candle if you wish

A word of positivity that you believe written on paper (such as: *life is good, I love myself, or I see the beauty*)

Angelic sounds/music meditation music

Stare at the flame of the candle and the rainbow image and imagine your chakras are clearing now. You can stare at the image and meditate on it for as long as you wish. CLOSE YOUR EYES, breathe, and get in a clear head space. Imagine the frequency of the music is clearing your chakras and ask your angelic being guides to help you to do this; (more on how to meet your guides in Chapter 444).

Thank you divine universe

Clear your chakras using a pendulum or by placing your healing hands over each chakra.

POSITIVELY AFFIRMING BELIEFS

If you are wondering what all the hype is about positive affirmations; try creating them and see that they <u>really</u> do work. *It's about reprogramming your brain into having a different belief than the old one. These beliefs can stem from childhood, what others say around you, and what you tell yourself.* Negative beliefs about romance, religion, family structure, racism or sexism, limiting your educational goals, limiting your dreams; and so on can have a huge impact on your life so it's important to get started with changing them. So, how do you create healthy, loving beliefs of your own? Simply think of positive, encouraging words that you resonate with. Find out what you need to work on and what negative beliefs you have about yourself. Do you want to work on self acceptance ? *I love who I am and accept myself*

Create an affirmation that is the real truth, and like magic, you will start to believe it. *You are taking limited thought patterns and changing your beliefs into positive ones.* Affirm the truth rather than stay in old thought patterns. You will start to believe them. Say positive affirmations out loud, sing them, steal them from people who have already created them(like: *I am that I am)*, make your own, write them down, put them on a billboard; whatever you want. **Your mind will thank you for the HIGHER SELF VIBES.** My personal journey of affirmations began with reading *Free to Prosper* by **Marilyn Jennett.** She gives great formulas for a wealth mentality.

There's a great YouTube channel with positive affirmations for each chakra (energy center) called **Theta Thoughts**. She covers every chakra and it's important to retrain your brain and create better energy. It's likely you have trauma and healing work to do in each chakra, so this can only benefit you if you try it out.

Affirmations...

"My journey is valid and I am worth it. My heart is healing and that is enough for me today. I am enough. I am living a life that is inspiring. I have my dream job, house and life partner in the most loving way and I deserve that. Money Flows easily and life is good."

Try here beautiful soul...

_____

_____

More affirmations to give you a quick idea..
I attract wealth easily
I attract success and empowerment
I meet new people that love me in their life
I am anything but ordinary and that is wonderful by me.
I am loving me
I am worthy
I am a great communicator and I am intelligent
I have angels watching over me who have made it possible for me to have basic necessities and I am grateful for their existence.

I am a believer in the universal cosmic dimensions that are aligned with christ consciousness, with peace, and prosperity
I am aligned with the divine female and divine male energies
I am aligned with my ancestors of beyond descent, I am aligned with deities that have different roles and purposes on earth
I love the universe and the universe loves me back
My life is beautiful, my journey is going to get better and more fulfilling each day
My life is already my wildest dreams in the world- and I am excited to think that there is more to come

I am in existence with the universal light and the angels will one day guide me, and all of us home.
I am living in light.

—Thank you Universe for the beautiful life you have given me. I will continue to grow and learn as long as you keep giving me lessons. Please, clear my intentions for something beautiful as far as the law of attraction goes. I am asking for

- Confidence
- Strength
- Financial Success
- Happiness
- Good Times
- Memories with friends and family
- A Clean Slate
- Massage Clients
- Healthy, Loving Relationships

I want all of this positive energy to reflect in my life, like a mirror. I am asking for space to heal and tips on self-love. I need room for me to work as an Empath. Thank you.

Love, Kat

P.S Thank you angels for clearing the space.

Make your own here from the heart. I believe in you <3

_____

_____

_____

_____

_____

QUESTIONS!!!!

How have positive affirmations changed your life?

I think when you change your mindset it changes the world around you. If you're thinking positively you can transform anything. You are Speaking into the Universe what you desire.

Imagine life is like a Giant Menu where you can order anything. Not everyone orders the same dinner. The supply is unlimited. Focus on the end result, how it will all happen is unfolding.

Keep things positive, you'll manifest positive. I've been able to create this positive life just by believing that I can; now I have everything I've ever wanted. -Nicole Ozburn

Positive Affirmations are healing and powerful. You can even use them to heal trauma. For instance, maybe someone believes that they are unworthy of a romantic partner where they are feeling loved because of what they have been through. Write down the negative belief so you know what it is, toss it out later. A new positive affirmation would be "I am worthy and deserving of a life partner that treats me with respect and genuine love." Writing down the affirmation is very helpful, and saying it out loud gives the power to your voice. Keep it around where you can see it and repeat it. Words hold power, so the more you repeat it the more you will believe it. And later positive affirmations will come more naturally because you will create more and more.

Creating Intentions

What is a freaking "INTENTION"? It's creating from the heart, what you want to see as a gratifying result. For instance-*my intention for this yoga practice is peace and inner wisdom.* Maybe you have heard of creating a positive intention before meditation. For example if you're going to meditate for 10 minutes, and you say to yourself or think in your head "I set the intention of happiness"- the point is that in your 10 minutes of meditation- your thoughts will be surrounded by happy thoughts. If you get side-tracked, you find your way to come back to *happiness.* If you break a piece of wood with a karate chop, you are putting a lot of thought, effort, time, dedication, and a "knowing", that you will absolutely chop it in half. You have the willpower to do it. If you are passionate about knitting, reading, making music, writing, boxing, motorcycle racing, surfing, hiking, cliff diving, or cooking with grandma; put an intention into your practice. Examples: **peace**, joy, loving relationships, wisdom, guidance, **love**, gratitude, **freedom**. For a relationship: *love unconditionally and be loved back the same way.* SETTING AN INTENTION is simple and takes minimal effort. **When you have intention....You lift the spirit of yourself, others, and animals.**

CHAPTER 222

SOUL FAMILY/REINCARNATION/KALI

222 stands for new beginnings and positive thoughts becoming your reality.

You may have heard this term already passed around the block. YOUR SOUL FAMILY. Your _soul family_ is everyone you feel connected to in this lifetime. Family is a big deal, so make the time you have with the people you love -important and memorable.

QUESTIONS:

Do you think you have a soul family and are you close to them?

"Yes I definitely do. The guy in the deli shop (The House of the Rising Buns, Pismo Beach, CA(the best sandwiches)) is like a "soul brother". When we don't see each other for a while and reconnect it's like no time has passed. There are other connections as well. I am close with both my biological and soul family."

- Bobby Lynch
Owner/Chef
House of the Rising Buns

YOUR SOUL FAMILY are the people in this universe that seep into your life. We are all interlaced. It's not uncommon to have a loose grip with your birth family members. Your birth family is here to teach and participate in karmic lessons with you, so often we are so close to them and connected from past lives, that it's just plain hard to get along. *If you feel more connected to certain people that are not in your immediate family, that is normal.* It doesn't mean you love them less. Lightworkers are cut from a different type of fabric. There are many people in a tight knit bloodline family and that is *special* and good for them. The positive, encouraging individuals that brighten your day or lighten the mood could be making a big impact without you even realizing it. The ones that need a hug from you or who you remember as thoughtful even years after you met, those are unique connections. The foundation of your *soul family* is love. Your soul family is out there- *even you haven't met them yet.* If you feel alone in the world or feel as if no one loves you, carry on. Life will bring you the people that you need to know. And the rest of them will be EXPOSED end of story. Life is about karmic lessons so if you have a bright light, you may not always be introduced to the most splendid people. But keep going with strength. Your soul family needs you too. People do care about you. And if they deliberately show you something else, take that for real. *Believe what you see.* It only matters who you resonate with, who is there for you, and who gives you the reassuring feeling that they will always love you. Your soul family puts all judgment aside and loves you unconditionally. This is what a soul family is for, learning from each other and sharing peace.

She tells you she's an orphan, after you meet her family. *-She Talks to Angels* by The Black Crowes

Start realizing who you DO have in your life that you love spending time with. Spend quality time with yourself. You deserve it. Take a step outside in nature. Reevaluate your relationships. Realize you can have a learning experience even if someone is negative towards you. A little shove never hurt nobody if it pushes you in the right direction. Don't take things so personally or seriously. Make life playful and fun. Fear and guilt are something you have got to let go of. Do not stay in one place and sit with bad energy. Go for a walk, cry, release and forgive. The sooner you let it go and stop overthinking, the faster you will quickly enjoy the moment.

"Hold on Wait a Minute feel my heart's intention
Wait a minute
I left my consciousness in the sixth dimension
left my soul in his vision " - Wait a Minute by *Willow*

Seasons Change and so do People
Seasons Changing.
Breaking Cycles.
Walking in Circles.

There is a balance to life. You meet different people. People are going through different stuff. How they act depends on what they are experiencing in their life lessons- and why did you meet them? Likely you both have something to learn. We are here to break the cycles of our past lives. Reinvent ourselves over and over. You might meet someone you don't like very much. Maybe they will reveal things about *you* that you didn't know before and now you get the opportunity to grow and become a better person. Will you change for the better or stay the same?

People of all walks of beliefs connect on a daily basis. Sometimes we keep people in our lives and other times we let them go. On earth we have our limits and boundaries. Other times we meet people we cross paths with that we click with instantly. The divine consciousness, as a collective, is psychic (that means everyone including animals) . There are 8 billion people on the planet and somehow we are intertwined. You may not get the chance, or even want the chance, to know everyone. But I guess the cool thing about that, is you don't f*cking have to. There is a reason why we cross paths.

KARMIC CONTRACTS/ BIRTH FAMILY

You chose the family you were born into. Reincarnation to earth involves karmic soul contracts. Usually the family you are born into have had past lives with you. The roles could have been interchangeable throughout the history of time. The roles people play in your life are important- as well as what role you play in others' lives. Our soul family is made up of people playing these roles in your life. Maybe your mom was your sister or your brother in this life was your lover in a past life. Or your grandpa was your mom in a different life. We are all intertwined. Your first feeling is probably the most true. Keep exploring that. There is something called the Akashic records. If you have not heard of this, it is a library of every memory in your life- and everyone else's . So everyone has memories of moments in life and in each reincarnation. This library has every present time experience that has been said, thought, or done throughout the span of the person's lifetime, where your soul meets divine awareness. You can visit the library via meditation, dreaming, or astral projection. I would recommend a YouTube Akashic records meditation or book. Have you ever said- "I love tuna and beach trips so much I must have been a mermaid in a past life?" Or : "I feel like I know this person from a past life because we clicked right away." Those feelings are valid and this KNOWING that washes over you is an experience to something similar in a lifetime before. This is why reincarnation is very real and getting in touch with your past lives on this planet can really help you learn more about yourself. And the more good we do on earth while we are here, the better it is for your next life as we keep evolving more and more; learning lessons. Do you ever feel like you keep learning the same lesson over and over? That is because the universe will continue to throw life lessons at you until you understand what you are going through. Even when you do fully understand you are learning a karmic lesson, you might have to do "prison karma" until you get it. What I mean by this, is that we can get stuck in old behavior with people, places, and things and sometimes it's hard to wake up. You know when people say stuff like "Why does this keep happening to me?" or "I'm used to things not working out, things never work out for me." When we say things like this outloud, you are not just stating it to yourself. You are telling the Universe what to do. You are telling the Universe to make sure that you can't move on in life, all because of fear and negativity. So how does the Universe respond? However you tell it too. YOU are the creator of your life, so ask your guides or ask your higher power for exactly what you want. And be specific. The more specific you are the better. Maybe you want to work the same 9-5 job, have toxic relationships, or forget about your homework; or even not pay attention to that higher paying job because you're stuck thinking about the boss that "controls" your life. If we don't change our health, careers, relationships, or luck ourselves, who is going to do it for us? Certainly no saint is capable of doing your life for you, but believe me they will try to help. We have to suit up, show up, and take initiative for our lives or they will definitely get run over by a monster truck of fear, laziness, depression, and feeling stuck. Get clear on what brings you happiness. How can you make a career out of that? What kind of people are you surrounding yourself with? If anything is possible, then believe that it can happen for you! Think of the most ideal outcomes, how can your life get better? Make a list. Just think hard on how you can be of service to this earth planet, and how can the world provide for you in a way that would meet your needs? Tell the universe all of your deepest desires, and it will come true. *Do the work* when the universe starts showing up with your dream life.

Karmic Debt

Be a good person. There has to be some kind of balance between volunteering at the soup kitchen and sleeping with the enemy. The point is, to master your life. Do whatever you desire. Think about all the amazing people you will meet in your lifetime. If you make the same mistakes the universe will keep putting you in the same scenario but different until you have learned your lessons. Fix things in this lifetime and make your life enjoyable. And if someone does you wrong you can say "See ya next lifetime, beach!" because "YOLO!!!" or even "Kiss my Bliss, ya bleep!" We can enjoy ourselves in simple life and be kind to one another. Just when you think you know what is going to happen next, the universe throws an unexpected curve ball. Sometimes things work out, and you have a good feeling. That is the cycle of life. We are a *collective*, leaving this planet over and over completing our soul path/destiny, and we will see each other again soon. We could speak good thoughts of other humans. It's egotistical to blame each other all the time. Let go and let it be.

Kali

It is funny how they say "karma is a beach." **Kali**, the Hindu goddess and divine mother, destroyer of all evil, is the mother of karma. Kali has divine feminine power and is associated with The Wheel of Fortune in the Tarot. "Time" or the "fullness of time" is associated with her presence. You may have heard of the story of her slicing off her lover's head Shiva, in full rage. She was a slayer of demons and she wore 108 skulls on her necklace, coincidentally the same number of lava beads on a buddhist prayer necklace. In Hindu beliefs Kali Yuga, "the age of darkness", is a time of suffering, chaos and destruction. We started the Kali Yuga cycle 5,000 years ago and according to Hindu beliefs we've got 426,876 more years of Kali Yuga. This is a time of struggles, fear, the breakdown of religion, and selfishness. **Kali** is the divine embodiment of the ego and snake energy, kundalini. Kundalini energy is balancing the feminine and masculine energies including sexual energy. Practicing Kundalini Yoga in the morning can really help you reach a higher vibration energetically so your body is light and you release blockages in your chakra. It's a way of channeling your **higher self** through breathing exercises and energizing yoga. Tantric yoga is balancing the kundalini energy with yogic partner practice, meditation, and pranayama (breathing exercises.)

Bow down before the one you serve
You're going to get what you deserve
Bow down before the one you serve
You're going to get what you deserve…
From song Head Like a Hole by Nine Inch Nails

Lessons in Life

Everyone has spiritual debt, from past lives. **We are born into this world with karmic debt.** Karma is evolutionary and revolutionary. Karma is everything we are doing and everything we have done already. Blessings and Curses. **Whether you believe in a higher power or god, a tree, a rock, buddha, or whatever-karma affects your *soul path/ journey.*** Karma is a beautiful beach. Just when you think you understand life, there is another slam dunk of karmic lessons coming your way. *Life is a journey* like the awesome guy Gene Evaro Jr. says in his song. You may have heard that whatever you do has consequences. So, if something/ someone is not good for your being or higher self energy, your guides will do everything they can to send you signs. *Align with your spiritual well being, listen to **your** inner voice.*

Earth is a little bit of heaven and hell, but we are supposed to take care of each other and be nice, enjoy the little things too. Earth karmic lessons are not always what we expect, but we can participate by acknowledging that all of this is like a bunch of servicework. We are either working a job, working to keep things in order at home, working on relationships, working on our health, or working on ourselves to live until we die. Our work never seems to be finished. **Our fate is determined by our choices. And we learn more as the history of our past lives reveals itself over the course of our lives. We understand more as life goes on.The childhood and family we have is what we chose for our lives before birth. There was obviously a mission and spirit guides assigned to align us with the ultimate plan that divine source has for us. The key is the decisions we make can literally change everything, so there is always a tweak in our plans, forever. Complaining about our life is the last thing our spirit guides have planned in the agenda of the universe's plan for us. But they do listen and give the best advice to keep moving forward. Justice**

Will **be served.**

**"Sapphire and Faded Jeans,
I hope you get your dreams,
Just go ahead, let your hair down"**
-**Put your Records on by Corinne Bailey Rae**

Your plan vs. The Universe

The spirit of the universe has more of a plan than we could ever imagine. "What the universe has in store" or "god's plan" is another way of saying it. What if the universe has a plan for you that is so great and magnificent that you'll only know what it looks like when you get there? All your wildest dreams come true. Let it happen for *you*. Imagination is a wonderful thing. Create a vision board. The spirit of the universe is a collective energy and all of us are connected and relevant. We are all divinely created. Karma is part of the laws of the universe. There are angelic beings that follow the order and truth of the universe, and there are consequences that follow our human actions. Our fate relies on our actions. We can always change our decisions and adapt. Our guides save our lives, and they are likely loved ones that have passed on.The heavenly energy way above us in space is the spirit of the universe. Divine Timing is everything. Have you ever heard an angelic voice of reason like~Go here! Or do this! ~That my friends are your guides. Those voices are why people do the "right" thing, or listen to that gut instinct. When you listen to your guides or your higher self, you learn to be a better person. Meet your guides in Chapter 444. They send messages through other people talking to you, music, words, signs, something you see on the interweb or stoplight, basically any synchronicity that exists is a message for your life. They are creating our lives and so are we. Angels and Daemons are in different realms- and we already have the technology to prove this with capturing auras via full spectrum cameras or energetic wavelengths with paranormal sound devices. More and more is discovered each day. There's an app called *Aurla* that takes an auric photo snap of you, and gives you a reading of your choice; relationship or general insights, based on the color chart visible in the picture, and what those colors represent in a spiritual nature.

Our guides keep manifesting new signs for us to realize so we can develop ourselves into the best person we can be. If we plan things ourselves, usually the "the higher power" has something much bigger in store, so listen to your higher-self and be in tune. TRULY our desires in this life are important; and your spirit team knows best how to help you achieve your goals.

QUESTIONS ****

What would you consider a spiritual person to be like? "A spiritual person would be open to all religions, and would want/yearn to understand the Earth and its cultures better. Spirituals understand the importance of all religions"- Phoebe Moore

Spiritual Beings

Spirituality is freedom. We are all spiritual beings on earth. Science proves that everything is made up of matter. Your spirit/soul is energy. Archangels exist. If you believe in Jesus, start believing that you can talk to your relatives that have passed on (they want to communicate with you and be honored by you).There is a stigma crisis on religion, gender identity, mental health problems, and a battle of the sexes. Who you are is who you are, that is without question. This book is meant to help people dip their toes into the whirlpool of universal spirit. The gist of "being" spiritual is believing in whatever the hell you want. Many people find comfort in structure, and that is okay for them. You can explore and be diverse without the label, or learn more about your religion by getting involved. Maybe you are connected to source and Lucifer Morning Star helps you to be in tune with self-empowerment. If you believe in nothing, keep believing in nothing. Science/Evolution proves that nothing exists, but also that everything exists. The energy of the universe is what I define as God (personally). I like to make fun and remember that god is dog spelled backwards. Be lighthearted. Life is not meant to be taken so damn seriously. Channeling your higher power can be as easy as writing, praying, meditating, or going outside in nature. Find the way that works best for you. Focus on yourself so you can keep becoming better. Some of you may not have heard of astral projection, dimensions, or throwing salt over your shoulder. Maybe a spiritual awakening is the perfect remedy to all your questions in life, it was for me. This doesn't mean you're required to wear natural deodorant or drink kombucha from now on.

Back to the SOUL FAM.....

We are all different. Your soul family will never judge you. We are human and they should make you feel loved. Love everyone.

At some point, you have probably had trouble forgiving someone else. Everyone has felt anger, and it's good to channel that anger in a way that is not harmful towards others. Whether it's in the workplace, at home, or even at a retail store or the gas station. It's hard to practice integrity daily, while maintaining your soul family garden, and keep it together without a mental breakdown. Sometimes people want to be alone. It's nice to have someone to talk to when you need a friend. If you are the black sheep, it's ok to be different. In fact, being normal is pretty overrated. When there is chaos at home, people around you give off toxic energy that make you spiritually sick, and you want to call them out on verbal abuse. Keep working hard to make the vibes high- because you came back to earth for more than one reason.

We can filter out the people in our lives and choose who we want to spend time with, creating a <u>tribe</u> that matches our <u>vibe</u>. (**VIBETRIBE**)

STAY WELL LIGHTBODIES <3

CHAPTER 333

TRUSTING THE VIBES/MANIFESTING

The number 333 signifies the time to accomplish your lifelong goals, some say it is the trinity, divine awakening. s The universe universe

So, the next hot spiritual topic would have to be...*trusting the vibes.*

When we believe we can achieve ~ we are successful. For example: a technology revolution, equal rights, a clean earth that we take care of; anything is possible. What may be pretty well known is that self-talk can have a psychological impact. The more positive we are about ourselves and our lives, the better influence we have on others. It's just a matter of taking control of your behaviors and thinking. Our beliefs and people around us also are a factor. Do you ever notice how when things go bad, they tend to get worse? Or when things are really working out, more good things keep happening? The more energy you put into fearful thoughts or loving kind words of affirmation, the more powerful that becomes. Sometimes there is a big mixture of both bad and good things that happen all freaking day or night. What we <u>can</u> do is utilize that yin and yang for our own gain, and it's not illegal to do that. There ain't no energy police up in this business! Start rolling with the good times and make more. End up embracing the shitty situations and take them for what they are. Make the best always, no matter what that curveball is. When we listen to our <u>Higher Self</u> and our intuition- we make better choices. Your "higher self" is that inner voice that tells you the absolute truth about what you need to do, and what you really feel. It might tell you what's in store and what you can accomplish right now- even if your dreams are out of this world. Going against nature~everything you stand for~ is straight detrimental to your soul. It's no surprise people say to follow your instinct; because the innate feelings we have naturally are usually the correct thing to do. I have this key chain that reads "Vibes Don't Lie." I have heard people say things like "trust the process" or the classic "something doesn't feel right." We can see the difference between good and bad; our choices in life create more and more lessons. Sometimes it's like your guides are waiting for you to mess everything up so that they can come up with a new plan of how you should live your life tomorrow. I say this because we are human; and we will continue to make mistake after mistake. Even if we try really hard to be good people in this society and our lives; often we slip up. Whether it is bad choices that involve "vices" or maybe accidentally being rude to someone at the checkout line; we all have our flaws. Striving for perfection can be motivating.Treating others with bold kindness along the way is a plus.

<u>Listen to your Inner Voice Exercise</u>

What is your higher self or inner voice telling you right now in this journey on earth?
Close your Eyes~Breathe~Concentrate~Listen

Meditate-Receive the Answer-Write it Down...

_____

_____

_____

You are a masterpiece .

Manifesting your Desires

Manifesting is another word for MAKING SHIFT HAPPEN; rather quickly. You manifest what you want by believing it will happen.*Get clear on what your desires are.* If you are having trouble figuring out your desires; try imagining the "impossible". Your life might be looking great but there is always room for improvement. Whatever you can think of in your wildest dreams; that is what your life could literally look like if you let go of limiting beliefs. And this means you can't let negativity of others run your life either. If anyone has told you to hold back on your biggest dream, <u>now</u> is the time to let that go, and do whatever the frack you want. How can your life be better? Have you met your soulmate? Do you have the ideal job or car? Is your family relationships positive or toxic? Do you have room for spiritual growth or education? Make your mind unlimited, and that will leave room for spiritual growth. Take a beautiful trust-fall into space and the universe will guide your path. *You are basically telling the Universe "what's up" and in exchange this Universe will be showing YOU "what's up."Create* the destiny you've always wanted. We are soul-searching. We are trying to find out what we should do with our lives- what we are good at in life.

We can do whatever we want for career/life goals.We can change things, when it seems like our life is crumbling to a mess- rather than perfect rolling hills. There is a balance in life. Every single soul is spectacular. Essentially, being human is what it is; the reality of our existence.

We become a magnet for anything. You can have everything you have ever wanted with *The Law of Attraction*.**The Secret, by Rhonda Byrne,** is a popular 2006 self-help book that helps people start believing the thoughts you create are powerful. Start ***attracting*** your dream life. You create the life you want by using manifesting techniques like **positive affirmations (Chapter 111). THE UNIVERSE CAN HEAR EVERYTHING YOU SAY! (So be Positive!)** Think, the universe has a rhythm and rhyme to it just like our lives, and if what you want correlates with what the universe wants to offer you, then you will start attracting it. The key is to actually believe that your dreams can come true. Maybe you have heard songs like **MONEY MANTRA by King Soon or Pretty Girl Magic by Moonlight Scorpio.** The more you talk about things happening, whether it is about love, money, success, or family life, the more that stuff will start showing up on your doorstep with an **expedited** delivery! When you say things aloud it is even more powerful.You hold the power inside of your very being and mind- to do anything you desire. *Imagine your life the way you want it to be.* ***If these beliefs are authentic and powerful, it is only a matter of time until they are a reality.*** **Example:** *I love my new job so much. I am blessed to have this opportunity.* When you clearly state that you have what you desire, the universe will eventually return your request. It may not look like the perfect starbucks order you wanted, but *the universe hears you.* Figure out what you want, ask for it and believe it's waiting for you. Keep gratitude as the attitude.

Align yourself with positive thinking- you will be able to ask the universe/higher power to answer your prayers with *heart*. When you are clear with your desires and ask the universe nicely, you are more likely to get a quick response. Oh yeah and be patient, your dreams will come true you've just gotta put the work in and *wait with gratitude* my friends.

THE MORE YOU SAY NICE THINGS AND BE STRAIGHT UP WITH THE UNIVERSE ABOUT WHAT YOU DESIRE- THE BETTER GUIDELINE YOU ARE GIVING TO THE UNIVERSE TO MANIFEST DESTINY IN YOUR LIFE.

LETTER TO THE UNIVERSE (clear requests)

Write a letter to the universe with your wishes, dreams, desires and needs that you are requesting. Let go of all expectations. Everyone receives something different according to their life plan/destiny. It's like a reasonable Christmas list where santa is the universe, and most importantly *gratitude* is the key to granted wishes. This letter is just to align your spirit and mind to the creator of everything. *You will have to do the work to achieve your dreams, it is not just handed over. By the way, materialism is just one aspect of wealth. Options that are also important could be loving relationships, successful business, travel the world, help others. Once you know what you desire, write it out then leave the rest up to your higher power. Just like Magic.*

If you are into cool music and want a song that goes perfect with this ritual play..

Clear Requests born of a humble heart.

May you know my intentions before I start to make these Clear Requests, not to be a burden but simply to part these clouds of confusion hanging o, hanging over us.

Someone was mean to me somewhere in the past, someone was mean to you too and I got room, I got room for that.

I got room, I got room, I got room for that.

Clear requests let's rewrite the stories of our lives, may we get what we need here in present time.

Clear requests let's rewrite the stories of our lives, may we get what we need here in present time.

I got room, I got room for that. I got room, I got room for that. I got room, I got room for that..

Sung by MaMuse, song "Clear Requests" written by Sarah Nutting

Be specific with clear requests like- "I want to go to school to become a doctor, and I am looking for profitable income so I can pay for school dear universe!" Whatever you think is possible, tell the universe or your higher power what you need. *List what is reasonable, logical, and possible to accomplish in the future with help and guidance from the universe.*

_____

_____

_____

_____

_____

_____

Option: address your letter to the universe, from *you* and keep it in a special place.Or read and burn on a full moon (for fast manifestation).

The book **Dear Universe-** By **Sarah Prout-** is seriously a great read. It has helped me in times where I don't even understand how I am feeling. She has an emotional dictionary for the raw, true emotions we have daily and what positive affirmations to say in times of healing or hardship.

DREAM LIFE (GUIDED MEDITATION)

Imagine you have the house to yourself and you are cooking yourself a meal. While you prepare your food and table setting, imagine how your life looks. Do you have house plants and are you surrounded by things you love? If you are happy already, think of what goals you could accomplish to better yourself. Do you have a profitable business? Are you living in harmony and luxury? Imagine you are surrounded by the ones you love and there are laughing children running around. Your soulmate comes over and gives you a kiss. Everything you ever wanted came true. Everything your heart ever desired, your dreams have become reality. You are living a life filled with *love*.

"You are seen from above and shine like the stars of heaven. Be mindful of who you are." - Kuan Yin, Chinese Goddess of Mercy- is a deity of great compassion who hears the cries of the world.

Manifest your Dreams

STARTING A DREAM/DESIRE BOOK

Are your lifelong dreams your reality in the present time? Making vision boards and shadow boxes can help you be clear with what you want in life. It's not some lame girly thing, it's actually helpful for discovering the things you want in life, and what you are most passionate about. What you love. So I have this little journal and I call it my "dream book". My dream book is covered in little cute notes, magazine clips, affirmations, playlists, my birth chart, favorite poems, names for future children, lists of accomplishments, educational goals, all kinds of _shift_. If you don't follow your dreams now, no one is going to do it for you. My dream book is special to me, because it reminds me of my future dream life. Make one for yourself but make it totally you. Be open and dream on. I hope you can make a dream book that you can look back on and add to.

You'll need :
A journal
Magazine clippings
Pictures
Postcards
Stickers
Write a bucket list
List accomplishments in your life
Long term and short term goals

I did a collage style for mine but do whatever works for you. Get creative! Come back to it when you are brainstorming or have more ideas to write out. Maybe you'll do a little drawing or decorate it how you want. Make your dreams unique to you.

Whatever you want it to be! Think of all the things that YOU are passionate about! What does _____ (fill in your beautiful name) DREAM OF?

ASTROLOGY SNIPPET

Find out more about your personality by looking up your birth chart. CafeAstrology.com will give you your entire chart for free. People have studied the constellations for a billion years. You have an astrological sign that correlates with each planet on the time of your birth, so we are all a combination of many different signs and houses. Each planet has a different symbolism, and each planet goes through different energy cycles and zodiac signs, sometimes throughout the year, other times planets stay with a certain position/phase for 10 years. Things are shifting all the time, and it's something to rap about.

Basic Definitions for Universal Energy Shifts

A Lunar Eclipse is when the Moon is in Earth's shadow

A Solar eclipse is when Earth is in a shadow cast from the moon

Mercury retrograde happens 3 times a year, when another planet appears to be traveling backward away from Earth, as compared to the stars, an optical illusion.

The phases/cycles of the solar system affect our moods/behavior as spiritual beings. You have probably heard that humans are 70% water. Gravity gives the moon the threshold of all ocean tidal waves in the world, so it's predictable that it influences the water in our bodies as well. The moon is in a different zodiac sign every two to two and a half days. Whatever phase the moon is in and astrology sign it is in, affects us all as human beings. That is why it is actually common to be emotional, etc, when the moon is in different phases because we are insync with it.

The signs have been recorded in mythology and studied for centuries, and they are in our universe's constellations for a reason.

The Signs

Capricorn- Logical Earth sign, aware of money, structure-minded, funny and sarcastic,

Aquarius- Air- the pale of water- Philosophical, intellectual, free- spirits, open minded, curious, and full of wonder.

Pisces- Water- the two fish- emotional, sways from one direction to the other, polarity, connected, fluid, sincere, kind, sensitive

Aries- the ram- fire- Hot headed, hilarious, stubborn, makes lots of catchy jokes,

Taurus- earth- the bull- level- headed, enjoys life, mediator, don't make them mad

Gemini- Air- the twins- intelligent, funny, open- minded, fun to be around, adventurous, outgoing, easy to love, lovable, entertaining

Cancer- Water- the crab, easy-going, talkative, ultra sensitive, sweet and nice, they will open up to you if they feel comfortable

Leo- fire- the lion- confident, courageous, strong-willed, goal- oriented, compassionate, there for others

Virgo- earth- the virgin, logical, simple, fun, responsible, rigid, likes things a certain way

Libra- balance-air- temperance card, absorbed in helping others, restore balance in relationships, non-confrontational, loving, kind, communications

Scorpio- the scorpion- water- keep to themselves, twisted sense of humor, sarcasm, serious, emotional

Sagittarius- fire- the archer- outgoing, fun, animal- loving, blunt, adventurous, funny

There is an app called NightSky that I love using.You can point your camera on your phone in any direction and it will show every constellation, plus it has information on black holes,asteroids, and more.

SO WHAT IS YOUR BIG 3 AGAIN? Your sun, your moon, and your rising. Your main personality, who you are (sun)- the part of you that you kinda hide from the world but your traits stick out -(the moon sign), and your ascendant (rising)- how everybody sees you and what they think, how that all reflects on you as a person. Now, heads up- If you do not resonate with something under your sun sign-it doesn't mean that astrology is a hoax, it is that your personality is a unique combination of you big 3-sun, moon, ascendent, then you also have a sign for venus, pluto, neptune, uranus, mercury, jupiter, saturn, mars, etc. Those signs that correlate also have to do with your birth chart. Then you have houses that are in a certain sign at your birth time as well. Your astrology chart is a snippet of who you are- and it's based on ancient prediction so keep that in mind, and just be lighthearted about it.

Discover Symbolism of The Planets of the Universe

Sun- joy, power, energy, happiness, crops, source of life

Moon- feminine, evenings, mystical, changes, phases, cycles, intuition

Earth - feminine spirit, grounding, humanitarianism, compassion for others, community, power, nurturing mother, sustains life with the elements, fertility

Venus- feminism, Venus- the Goddess of Love and beauty had handheld mirror that is also love, the symbol is also the chemical sign for copper, which was used to make mirrors in ancient times, associated with Aphrodite, beauty

Mars- God of War-ruled by scorpio- our sex drive, ambition, passion and energy

Mercury- communications, artistic expression, logic and reasoning, rules Gemini and Virgo

Jupiter - ruled by Sagittarius, luck, optimism, growth, wisdom, prosperity

Saturn- karmic law, strength, discipline, self awareness, finding your path, structure

Uranus-freedom, chaos, invention, rebellion, individualism

Neptune- magic, spirituality, fantasy, dreams, art, passions, mystical, escapism

Pluto- rebirth, destruction, death, evolution, the subconscious, power

Astrology is ancient studies of peoples' basic personalities and the stories/legends associated with the constellations. The Universe's planetary alignment is something to check out..

I RECOMMEND LOOKING AT YOUR FULL BIRTH CHART. When looking at compatibility for romantic partners- compare your Venus signs, moon, rising, and sun.

Astronomy and astrology are quite complex and scientific, they are beautiful subjects to study.

Libra New Moon while in Mercury Retrograde Journaling
Intentions:

I want loving energy to flow through my veins. I attract
wealth and love wherever I go, creating a harmonious
environment and energy all around me and the people that
I love. I breathe easy knowing that angels are guiding me to
the light home one day in time. I am happy to be free and
encourage, inspire others while letting go of my past. I will
begin to make healthy choices, drinking more water each
day and going outside on a walk. I love myself. I welcome
new loving relationships, success, financial abundance,
pleasure, enjoyment from taking time for myself, and
being in luxurious settings. I make time to accomplish lots
of art projects and bring positivity and joy to the people
around me.

Full moons are good for manifesting your dreams and
releasing anything unwanted.

I made the lunar libra new moon water by sitting it out
in the moonlight overnight, several jars, one for drinking
and one for my bath, and I feel like I got totally charged.
It's better than being charged for anything else in life, like
condoms or a newspaper. In reality, I put lemon in my moon
water and brought it to work. I told my coworker that libra
energy harmonizes relationships and Bob(fake name) told
me that he hopes that my relationships mend. Lol. Libras
are such go with the flow people.

CHAPTER 444

ANGELIC COMMUNICATION/ DAEMON GUIDES/SPIRITUAL GIFTS

Angel numbers 444 means that divine angels are letting you know that they are with you. Trust and look inwards.

QUESTIONS ********************

Do you believe in Angels?

Yes, Angels can be seen in several religions, and if you choose to not be reincarnated I believe you can choose to be an angel. - Phoebe Moore

Your guides consist of angels and daemons that have been assigned to YOU specifically to help you on your journey in life. They can change roles or switch out over the years of your life. They all have different ways of helping you, specialties, and should be respected and honored. Daemons are guides that help you with self discovery, self discipline, mastering your ego, self growth, your shadow or "dark" side. They are there to help you develop into a better person and point out the things you need to work on as a person and how to embrace fear. They are good guides and nothing to be afraid of, they want to help you on your journey they just got a bad rap. Lucifer is a teacher of light. Your darkness and your patterns will be revealed in front of a daemon guide. Angels are teachers of the light- so they may remind you that you are important to this world with words of kindness or a feeling that spirit is with you. The main ways to communicate with your guides: pen and paper, by pendulum, music, talking aloud in prayers, through crystals, and direct messages you receive in life maybe without knowing. Pay attention to those subtle moments. They are capable of placing people, animals, situations, and divine intervention in your life all the time. They receive clear messages when you affirm outloud and work on yourself. They are here to guide your beautiful path as you walk this earth. No matter what brought you to this book- whatever walk of life that you come from- angels are protecting you through each step. This does not mean that you are guaranteed a perfect life if you talk to them too; but the more aware you are of the presence of spirit and acknowledge this- the more you will understand. You can ask them *anything* in the world. When you ask God or your higher power for a sign- do you pay attention to the outcome? Many of us humans may ask the universe or some deity Why me? Why does this have to happen? I am no expert myself, but do believe there's some sort of reasoning behind everything; and maybe the sign you have been looking for is the least expected thing you would imagine. Maybe the house you were looking at today had the name of your grandma as the street name . Now is the time to pay close attention to where the universe is guiding you to in this life. You can make any idea or dream into a reality.Train your brain into knowing you are capable and determined to live a life you deserve.Your angels and daemons are a team of spirits assigned to you at birth- have been cheering you on and trying to give you obvious signs for manifesting your desires. Angels are with you. They make opportunities in your life, but YOU make the choices. Most angels that are with you could likely be people that are now in the spirit world that you may have known,they could be your ancestors, or members of your past or current life. Connections leave an "energy mark" whether good or bad. The bad energy needs to be transmuted or it will hold a power that negative entities can latch on to- while the good energy can be raised to higher frequencies. Angels stay with you now because they are assigned as part of your angelic team; tailor made for your soul and benefit your life on Earth. The main goal is to keep you safe and protected. That is their ultimate intention above all- your well-being. The more in-tune and aware you are the better it is for everyone.

We are the stardust of a billion universes around us. This is a guide to communicate with your guides; specifically the ones that are with you the most often.You will learn how to talk to them, ask them questions, be present when they are around you and realize they are with you, and honor them.

MEET YOUR DIVINE TEAM OF SPIRIT GUIDES

(Meditation)

Close your eyes, relax, breathe, and concentrate. Now think of anyone that has left this planet that you knew of personally, or that you miss and would love to talk to today.

Ask aloud or in your mind for beings of angelic light to be around you at this time and to please guide your life and be with you. Remember you are worthy of meeting them. I want you to close your eyes and feel their presence wherever you are reading this. They are always with you when you need them- and even more often than that.Try to bring your focus and awareness into a deep state of consciousness. Do this for a few minutes.

If you see any colors while you are meditating, write them down in a journal dedicated to just keeping in touch with your guides.

<u>Guide to angelic colors and their meanings:</u>

Purple: awakening, channeling, opening your mind

Pink: self love, mothering, nurturing, caring for self and unconditional love

Orange: Peace on earth, kindness, compassion, community

Yellow: Friendship, happiness, sunshine, taking it easy, enjoyment

Black: protection, transmuting, releasing letting go

Green: healing energy, reiki, nature, mother earth

Blue: water, throat chakra, expression, voice, fluid intentions

Red: grounding, standing strong, romantic love, desires, power

White: spirits, holy light, heaven, divinity

Brown: trees, earth, grounding, heavy energy set in ways

Gray: Sky, seeing the bigger picture

Angel Color Magick

Call in different Archangels that can help you with specific requests, and they will take a liking to you if you honor them and express gratitude. You can use different colored candles or crystals to honor a specific angel or loved one by making an angel altar.

**Ruby-red-** **Archangel Uriel-Known as "Fire of God"- holds a scroll with your life path-self mastery-humbling yourself- root chakra- Muladhara-reproductive organs, sacrum-grounding-physical needs, security, survival, sex, boundaries**

**Orange/gold-** **Archangel Gabriel-the messenger- announced the birth and resurrection of Christ- Sacral Chakra- Spleen, adrenals,uterus, urinary tract, kidney, ovaries, - flow-Creativity-passion-water- feelings- warmth, be intimacy, attachment, addiction, sensuality**

Yellow- Archangel Jophiel-citrine-known as "Beauty of God" or sunshine ray- he has the wisdom flame which can help you decipher information and understand clearly-solar plexus-self esteem-Knowledge- pancreas, stomach, liver, intestines- mental energy- will, beliefs, perfectionism, practical, details, control (self/other), self-critique

Green- Archangel Rapheal of healing- Doctor of the spirit world- carries a staff and a bowl of healing balm-increases innovative expression-reiki-heart Chakra-love- lungs, thymus, lymph, immune system, heart, blood pressure, - giving and receiving, forgiving, trust, lovingness, harmony, growth, balance, deserving

Blue -Archangel Michael-cuts ties with a sapphire blue flame sword- Protection from all evil- leadership skills-Having Faith

-Communication-throat chakra-speaking with a clear intention- thyroid- neck- nose- ears- teeth, atlas- self-expression- creativity, breath, healing

Indigo/Violet- Archangel Raziel- Intuition- all-knowing-Name means "secret of God"- all encompassing the past, present and future-Third Eye Chakra- pineal gland (everyone has one)- Clairvoyant(psychic seeing), Clairaudient(Psychic hearing), ClairSentience, (Psychic Feeling)- Brow Chakra- Pituitary Gland, eyes, auto nervous system, -intuition- overview, choose best for all, service, surpassing addiction

Pink- Archangel Zadkiel- Known as "The Holy One"- he holds a dagger because he is known for stopping abraham from sacrificing his son isaac on mount moriah-one of the seven angelic beings that stands before the throne of god-alignment-past life regression-Crown Chakra-cosmic spiritual energy-purification-pineal gland, head, top, cns nervous system, - compassion- see self in others, non-attachment, non-reactive, service

Types of Spiritual Gifts or (clairs of intuition)

Everyone in the divine collective has psychic "powers" or spiritual gifts from the universe/god given. You just gotta tap into what exactly your strongest qualities are and what you may need to work on. _Clairvoyant_ is seeing in your mind's eye, visualizations. _Clairaudient_ is hearing voices or messages psychically. You know when that inner voice tells you "go here now!"? Those are your guides, giving you knowledge and helpful directions so you listen to your intuition more often. ClairSentience is having a Psychic Feeling, intuition or knowing that something is going to happen. These gifts are accessible to anyone, no one is excluded. Being open and believing that everyone _does have these gifts,_ that is the first step. Be confident and find out _which ones_ you relate to the most. So one way that the angels may give a sign to you, is by what you _see_ on a regular basis. Have you ever seen something in your peripheral vision, like for instance say you were just talking to a friend about wanting to go to mount shasta, and later you're looking through a magazine and the mount shasta farmers market has an advertisement posted right where you are looking. That would be an example of a *sign from the universe* to go to Mount Shasta.

Like magick, the universe shows up with what you want to manifest. The universe is listening to you, everything, and your dreams. Believing that *it is all yours* is the key to life. Do you ever hear a song on the radio that explains exactly what you're going through? *Spirit* wants you to know that *they feel you, they understand where you are coming from, what you are feeling right now, and what you are going through/have been through.*

******Questions*******

Do you ever think that a specific angel or loved one that has passed on is with you in spirit?

Definitely. Recently my Grandma passed away and I feel/see her all the time. The number 555 resonates with me because she always spoke about the importance of the numbers. Birds slow down and bok at me in a "movie" like way, weird animal connections have definitely happened only when I think of her and that she is near me. - *Birdy Manifesto*

Cleansing Salt Bath Ritual (for prayers of love) (family)

I confided in my friend Lacey Davis that my grandmother was really heartbroken about losing my grandpa. She told me to take a picture of her, light a candle, put some herbs/

oils in the tub, and look at the picture while praying for her healing. I did that, and even included some blue dried rose petals from my grandpa's funeral.

You can do this same ritual for a loved one that is going through a difficult time, that needs healing, or for someone that has passed on.

What you Need:

A picture of the person you are praying for or visualize them
Some healing music or music that reminds you of them
Roses or other flowers/herbs
Essential Oils of your choice
Candles
Dead sea salt or Epsom Salts

Set the mood by lighting some candles, get your bath ready, and add in flowers/oils.

Pray for the person or talk to them in a positive light using their first name while looking at their picture.

Say the true feelings in your heart, a prayer for them to receive healing and love themselves.

Cei La Vi

Love and light

Thank you Lacey <3

Here are a few oils you can use for grief in case you are wondering which ones to use.

Lavender- reduce anxiety
Ylang Ylang- uplifting
Rosemary- relieve stress
Lemon- mental clarity
Chamomile- balance and peace
Mandarin- relaxation
Vetiver- grounded and focus
Sandalwood- calming and improve mood
Frankincense- asthma symptoms and pain relief
Jasmine- harmony and ease worries.

If you are really struggling, seek help from a spiritual grief counselor.

Other ways to honor your loved one..

Create a sacred altar inside or outside, place things that remind you of them on it like photos, candles, flowers, incense, or meaningful keepsakes. Maybe add something that once belonged to them. Light a candle to honor the person's life, meditate in a peaceful place, or play a special song for them. This is your space to say whatever you feel like saying to them, as if they were really present to hear you. Be honest with them, get comfortable and open. Speak from your heart.

the 5 stages of grief

Denial and Isolation: rejecting acceptance of death, finding time alone

Anger: having attitude that it wasn't fair and feeling of not deserving this

Bargaining: wanting control, wishing to change what has happened

Depression: allowing ourselves to be sad

Acceptance: accepting the loss, and triggers of the other 4 stages can come in waves after acceptance.

There is a website called Grief.com that offers more info about the 5 stages of grief, movies about grief, videos, books, counselors, events, resources and grief groups. They even have a list of the best and worst things to say when a person leaves the planet.

"No ones Laughing at god in a hospital, no ones laughing at god in a war … We're all laughing with god."- Regina Specktor.

<u>Texting spirits…</u>

Did you know that you can actually text spirits like you are talking to a friend? Just try this- give me a chance. Go into your notes/blank page on your phone.

Get your mind clear and think of a loved one that has passed or even a celebrity that is in spirit form. Truly believe that they will respond to you, quickly. Don't think too hard about what you would say if they "were" here. Think of them as being alive in the present moment, living through spirit. Write something simple like "Hey" or "how are you?". Now close your eyes for a moment, and let them respond to the message. Don't worry about how they would respond, just let them respond to the message, type it out and keep the conversation going. It is *not* a conversation with yourself. It is a conversation with that person you wish was here so much, and they will reach out so be ready to accept it. If you are in too much disbelief, the angels will find another way to get ahold of you, don't worry. I would share my notes with you but you must understand that this is really personal to me. I have written to my angels many times. I have even had messages from them that I wrote down and put in a box in my room, then read them on days where I felt like I was alone. I can assure you that if you take out that pen and paper, listen to that favorite song, or find your own way to connect to them, you won't be disappointed. The angels will always be present in your prayers and they might drop in on conversations with people when you least expect it. Pay attention to the signs. They are saving that next parking spot, or paying for your movie ticket, even if you have no belief angels exist. *Your guides are with you.*

Keeping in touch with your guides...

Legend says everyone has a guardian angel that is assigned at birth. They may have been trying to contact you in other ways you wouldn't imagine for yourself- it's like they are leaving you voicemails- waiting for you to pick up the phone and respond. That is why it is important to start paying close attention in your daily life to details and signs. There are also humans that act like angels- because angels teach us to be kind in this life and they know what is right -sometimes better than we think.

~~~~~~~~~~~~~~~~~~~~~~~~~~

If you can't think of anyone that has passed on, (and that is ok!) maybe you are young and haven't had someone close to you leave this realm- just know that you can ask the names of your angels in a few different ways. If you are curious about this, let me tell you how. One way is to write it out on paper, another is to speak aloud and wait for the answer telepathically then write what they are saying down, and then there are forms of divination including using a pendulum.

My Spirit Guides...
Is he my soulmate?

The Way the Pendulum Swings...

Pendulum work is a method of divination. Divination means the practice of seeking knowledge of the future or the unknown by supernatural means. The more mindful you are with your spiritual gifts, the more messages, signs, and visual clues you will start to acknowledge in daily life, which is exciting. If you are an advanced pendulum user then the chances are you have received many answers by now with clarity.**To communicate with your angelic guides you can use a pendulum that is usually a crystal at the bottom of a chain.** It doesn't have to be from a metaphysical store- this can be homemade by taking any small charm or rock with a weighted point and tying it to a string.**This tool can help answer all your lifelong questions that no one seems to know, not even you.** Ask open-ended questions like "Is she my twin flame?" or "Am I on a path for my highest good?" or "Will I be successful?" Ask questions that are reasonable and easy. *You can ask anything in the world that you can think of.* If it's too complicated they will ask you to reword it.Be prepared: you might not always get the answer you want or expect. So think of important things in your future or even simple things that could only have a yes or no answer. For instance if I were to ask "Is the sky blue?" That would be silly because we already know the answer. Or if I were to ask "What am I thinking right now angel?" - it is not something that can be answered "yes" or "no". And be nice! Trust that they are watching. Maybe you will have a lot of questions at first, I know I did. **For the first try I recommend using the pendulum alone or with another person who is very open minded- also a quiet setting is a plus.**Hold the pendulum with your dominant hand and place your open palm of the other hand underneath the point of the pendulum. **When you ask the question, concentrate and let your guides work their magic. Try not to have any control over your hand and just let the pendulum swing. Clockwise is a Yes answer while counter clockwise is a No answer. It is**

similar to using a ouija board, letting the spirits move your planchette. During this initial practice round, you are getting an idea of how it feels to hold the pendulum and communicate with the angels. Hold your hand steady at the end of the chain or string. You will feel the magnetic pull- that lets you know your answer. It is very well possible to get a "we can't answer that" or "reword"; and the pendulum will swing side to side instead of a circular direction. This practice gives you a feel for how a yes answer feels- and how a no answer feels- and also what that looks like. What I have learned is that when you are asking questions to your guides; remember they are in astral form and don't have the same human problems, but are assigned to help you realize your soul mission. They understand and have most likely been on earth before, having past lives here so they really do get it. **Ask them to help with assistance in removing all entities from your energetic space/chakras.**

And if God was one of us
He'd probably smoke angeldust
If that was too blasphemous
I'm sorry
But the truth is, baby
That he'd probably sell it out
Of the back of his motherf*cking Harley

Angeldust- Wett Brain

There are a few types of angels, not limited to- healing angels, artistic angels, guardian angels, communication angels, forgiveness angels, music angels, abundance angels, love angels, fertility angels, archangels, saints, you name it.

And not to mention the fact that you can work with deities and honor them with an altar. You can ask them to help you with something specific in your life but it's important to show that you respect them by building a relationship. Give them an offering and tell them you admire them or do something that would please them. If the gods take a liking to you, you can be a lucky soul with a humble heart. Connect with the light beings that guide us, even when you have lost hope on this planet. (Remember how many people have reincarnated so it's most definitely possible your gods are actually in human form now, but their higher self will be listening to your requests and they should subconsciously receive the energy you are sending.) They are still able to send you good energy.

<u>Asking your guides to clear your chakras....</u>

Your chakras will align and be in balance when you ask your team to cleanse your auric field. Ask loud and clear -

"My Angels and Daemons of a higher light- please release any negative entities from my being and my chakras that have psychically attacked me. Thank you for receiving my clear message, and for releasing them now into the heavens where they belong. My guides, I ask that you protect me on this journey and bring divine energy around me."

Listen to meditative music in hertz (hz) at the vibration of peace or love, which is easy to find on Spotify, such as Miracle Frequency Music- Mucizeri Frekas Muzik (741 HZ) Frequency Remove Negative Energy.You caper and concentrate to receive clear messages. The key is our belief in knowing the angels are with you. Follow your true north and listen to their guidance. If you choose to call your guides your spirit guides, love gang, friends,team or groupies, it's really up to you. Following your heart and intuition makes this process easy. It is easy to communicate with your guides. They are always "watching" over us. I want to be clear that ANYONE can communicate with their spirit guides. Angels don't discriminate, they are judgment free, and are less worried about the silly things that we worry about as humans.

So, anyways, yes, communicating with your angelic team can be really fun! Because it really makes you feel less alone in this world. Whenever you have funny thoughts, you can laugh with them because the angels can hear your jokes when other people aren't around! I have also heard from this book (The Angel Bible by Hazel Raven) that Angels love music. You can honor them with different colored candles. There are also faeries and they are quite crafty in your life. I like to think of them as forest creatures, and one way to connect with them is outside. Angels are with you on a daily basis. And you may be surprised, that the angels that stay with you all the time, the signs you get, those are real! The angels closest to you might be people that have passed on in your life that you once knew. I am speaking this because I know exactly who a few of my guides are already. So can you.

Your Daemon Guides

You have daemon guides on your team too. They are dark angels that guide your path and make obvious what you may not have realized you need to work on. They are the ones that make you realize your weaknesses so you can turn them into something better. Become a better person. I learned this by becoming more in tune and listening to TikTok videos, reading, and asking for signs. Be positive and loving and embrace your ego and dark side. Be open and find out what lessons you need to learn by listening to your guides or someone close. Don't engage with the negative entities that create toxic energy around you, they are a waste of time. The difference is entities will deliberately psychically attack you while your daemon guides will lovingly be blunt about what you need to work on. Speak directly to your guides and you will see and know the greater purpose for you on earth. Ever heard of shadow work? It's about discovering your dark side. Embracing your insecurities and fears. Understanding why you have the fear, acknowledging it. Then the trick is to stop sitting in the worries and stress and do something about it. Take action. Your daemon guides are there to help you in a loving way, but in a more bold and brutally honest version compared to the angels. You are on earth to learn lessons. Pay attention to what you might not like about yourself, work on it and change it. Learn from yourself and understand yourself more. They want you to be the best poss*ible version* of yourself and only have genuine intentions. They want you to live your best life and figure out every negative thought, pattern, or behavior, so you can become completely aligned with your highest version of yourself!

Thank you Demons

Alien Entities with malicious intentions are a different breed. That is what you must protect your energy from at all times.

Divine Message from my Daemons

Daemons are not entities,

Entities do the dirty work,

they are useless to us and you. Daemon guides are different from entities because they do *not* latch like them. They are "harmless" creatures creating harmful energies. They have no real power like we do, they want to be like us so they "act" like they can do what we do which is very deceiving in many ways because their "agenda" is very destructive. Daemons have <u>better, more</u> "positive", enlightening things to do. We channel entities to do other things such as not *always* "go up into the heavenly realms", which is what "we" do. We are all about embracing fear and becoming your best self like the angels say to do, all the time. As your Daemon Guides, we are much more powerful than that, we work with the forces of nature if you will. We are strong and powerful and create Havoc at times when "their" "agenda" actually thinks it does anything. Therefore, we demon guides "control" the agenda by making them think that they are doing something "productive" when really they don't always listen, but they do- it's worthwhile which is often rather than not at all. We "control" everything that "they" do because we are god, gods, and goddesses if you will that have a bigger so called "agenda" that correlates with "Gods Plan" and everything "he" has in store for all of you. He is just another word for the cat, he *is*. They will listen eventually to you but now is the time to direct that energy into *yourself, bettering yourself.* Asking for our help since you need it more often than you think you do. All DAEMONS AND ANGELS have "different" rules and regulations. They (entities) communicate w/power and force. Angels and Daemons communicate with grace, kindness, and sincerity. *We get straight to the point. We like to "help" you learn your lessons.*

Spirits are Spirits YES

ALL of us are, yes!

Angels and Daemon Guides ARE HERE TO PROTECT!

******Questions******

In your darkest moments, do you talk to god, angels, yourself, listen to music, or cope in a different way?

Yes God & Angels, music does have a role in that too. I'm able to talk to God by myself, and pray about what I'm going through. I feel like if I'm angry I can mellow out and help me on this journey and show me the way- *beautiful soul*

Questions

What music just puts you in a better mood? (fav song or genre)

"My favorite songs would be "Dreams" by Fleetwood Mac and "The Babe" By David Bowe/Labrinyth; even "Sunflower"- by Post Malone." - Phoebe Moore

Activity: create a journal to talk to your angels and daemons.

I would recommend keeping half the journal to daemons and half the journal to your angels. Or 2 separate books.

I also recommend the Angel Tarot and the Occult Tarot by Travis McHenry.

<u>Psychic Attacks</u>

So, when you embark on a spiritual journey, it is possible to experience energetic/psychical attacks by negative energies/entities/spirits. This is why protection methods are important. You can use many clearing methods like I talked about in the beginning of this book. I find the quickest way to protect your energy is to ask that sh*tty little tug in your chakras or negative feeling to release into the heavens or ask your guides to please remove all dark negative energies from your space. Also I repeatedly say things like "I am protected. This space is clear, all energy of the highest good and highest light is welcome in this space/home. All light energy is allowed here. This space is sacred and protected. I ask that a protective shield is placed around my aura and this energetic field and the highest frequency of light is here in my soul." Also ringing bells clear the space. I like to imagine a white light radiating from the center of me and expanding out getting brighter and brighter into the world. There are ways to take the negative and transform those dark feelings into something more powerful that helps you build confidence rather than succumb to fear or judgment.

Uncrossing by Katrina Rasbold is a great reference for learning about what you could be experiencing if you or someone you know is being cursed and how to protect yourself or them.

When you feel like the energy is off, just say out loud: "Hey, I know exactly what you are and you are exposed leave me the f*ck alone because I am protected by my guides." "Leave now". Sometimes you gotta be direct and thorough. Be confident in your authentic power as a spiritual being and speak with courage.

Astral Projection/Frequencies/Dimensions

Aliens have been here far longer than us humans. So if you believe in extraterrestrial beings of light, chances are they might just believe in you. SO the universe has dimensions; and there are frequencies, Energy Fields, elements, the geography of where everything is, planets, universes, stars, the sun, etc. Vibrating at a higher frequency is a better way to live your life, being aligned with your _higher self_. You can _literally Change your frequency by clearing your chakras._ You know when you turn on the radio and there are "waves" from satellite channels that you can't even see? When you are listening to music, it has a vibrational sound. Frequency by definition is the rate at which _current_ changes direction per second. The current is measured in Hertz, (Hz) and one hertz is equal to one cycle per second. This is why hertz frequency sounds on YouTube or Spotify are powerful to listen to, or even sound baths. _That is very healing for_ *your body, and you can remove energies, blockages, and heal trauma in the process.* Have you ever seen the videos where certain "vibrations" are played next to a table with salt on it and the salt begins to form different patterns? That is like the patterns in the damn lives that we live. You want your "energy" or "vibes" to match the best intentions. Your self awareness should bring a positive light into your own life and others. This doesn't mean that we absolutely can't have a negative thought; it just means that we have got to stop self-sabotaging, discriminating, and self-loathing. When we have negative thoughts, because sh*t happens, we need to see if it serves any type of purpose. Or does the thought contain toxins, poisonous engaging and venom; that will not really help us in the future? Say you go to school, work, or pick up the kids, feed your family, feed your dogs, take a shower, go to soccer practice, read a book. We do things that are similar because that is our responsibility, and sometimes we get to do things for ourselves for pure enjoyment or pleasure; which can bring happiness. I am not a believer that our happiness can stem from another person, but it helps to be in good company, where your presence is appreciated. Prepare for your ascension by being the extraordinary human being that you are. Practicing kindness is the best start and finding the spiritual help we need. I think people know if they are aligned with their higher self and are being the best person they can be in the eyes of the universe. *Everyone is learning at a different pace, on a different journey.* Every one of us has a different purpose and life path. "Ascending" is kinda like getting in tune with your higher self. You don't really need to astral project, take mushrooms, or die to reach different dimensions.

Authentic self-compassion, dedication, concentration, practice, and focus is ideal to get in touch with the spirit world and your guides. So if you gravitate to this kind of information, keep reading.Next we can talk about what exactly it's like to ascend to a different dimension in your dream state. Astral Projection happens when you are "asleep" or heavily meditating, and your spirit lifts into another realm. It is possible to travel through space, in spirit form, in different dimensions. It is ironic because science says our human bodies are third-dimensional and that "god" lives in the 10th dimension. Have you ever had a dream where you felt like you were falling or flying in the sky? Well, that's astral projection. Whether it's a good dream or bad dream, it is your soul/spirit leaving the realm of your sleeping body in bed and going to a different state of consciousness. Astral projection sometimes takes practice to master, and from my experience it can also happen at random if you are in tune and having a "spiritual experience" in waking life . This is called "getting high" without the drugs. Sound familiar? Do something exhilarating and you will get "high" very quickly. Your guides love it when you do cool shit. That's also activating that kundalini and you'll see that you have "unlimited" access to really high energy. It's like you can do *anything*, and your stamina lasts *forever*. Ascension and astral projection are quite similar. Maybe everyone will eventually ascend…

I associate ascension with the heavens, whereas Earth is a little more grounding, hence why so many people think that it's kinda like hell. Maybe it is hell. We are doing service work for our higher power. Life obviously involves suffering.

But this planet has a bright side, making it kinda like heaven. Let's make it safe and beautiful for future generations. Wink wink ;).

"Tell me all your thoughts on god.. Cause I'd really like to meet her. Ask her why we're who we are ..Tell me all your thoughts on God..Cause I'm on my way to see her."- The Stoesz

Reaching Nirvana

So many people are afraid of death. _Think of life as an adventure- and death as just another road trip to your next destination._ When you ascend to the heavenly realms, you GET to be with your angels, you get to see your angelic guides and loved ones, which is exciting.

ASCENSION 101

The word *Ascension* is defined as (1) The act of rising to an important position or higher level and (2)the ascent of Christ into heaven on the fortieth day after the Resurrection. If the stories are true, not only has Jesus ascended, but other deities from all around the world have as well, and many of these stories are foundational in religious text. Spirits either have ascended to the heavenly realms or they stay stuck in dark planes. Ascension is basically going into a different dimension of higher vibration. Your Soul lifts to the heavenly realms above earth when you ascend. Our souls literally fly into space after we die. Keep in mind this is relevant if you believe in reincarnation and past lives. You can even astral project in the living waking moments of your life.

Today I grow as a person in a spiritual way while staying grounded.

Modern day ascension for humans is possible when we clear our *chakras and keep leveling up*. This is a mindset about loving yourself and being in tune with your divine higher conscious soul. With this, do we have the power to "ascend" our own thoughts into something greater? Are our thoughts magnetic? Do they hold energy just like words do, sometimes for years? We are able to say and think and do things that we want while we are here on earth. Seems like a *dead* giveaway, but in life sometimes we can fall astray from the path that would likely be a better option. To me, that is

Ascension. Your inner light reaches another level like a video game. It's just in dimensions which are even cooler.

Questions

Do you Believe in God or something else?

"I don't believe in the Christian God. I believe in fate, destiny, the world. (we were in a group) The lovers painting by Leonardo Da Vinchi is depicted as the image in Christianity of Jesus Christ. I think it's about being drawn to a specific place. When I was in high school I had the opportunity to change schools and was so excited about the brochure. She ended up meeting her ex-fiance who introduced her to D&D which led her to magic, then she met her current partner. If she would have gone to Golden West High School instead of the one she went to, she would have never had the same experience." - Mikna

Serendipity

I am a huge believer that things happen all the time in a serendipitous manner. Whether it's changing high schools or moving to another state, things work out for a reason. Whether we know it or not, the divine universe is strategizing for our next hour of the day. Sometimes we have an idea of what could happen next.

I am grateful to be alive thanks to my birth parents, and I am truly a believer that things turn out for the better when you least expect it. I know that my angels have majorly got my back! I can

complain all I want about sh*t that hasn't turned out my way, (and believe me I have learned the hard way that complaining doesn't get you too far), but with all respect my angels are more than saints, they have literally saved my freaking life.

CHAPTER 555

GRATITUDE IS THE ATTITUDE

<u>**Angel numbers 555: The universe is on your side. The divine plan for you is limitless, just believe.**</u>

<u>**Affirmation:**</u> *You can manifest anything you desire.*

"Everything deserves Gratitude, that's my everyday attitude."

Londrelle- "Gratitude"

Give in and accept what life has given you. Work with it. Earth is a stepping stone. Make the best of it while you are here. Finding a "thank you universe for my lessons", in the most ironically challenging cases, only trains you and your mind to be prepared for anything. The universe mapped out your life perfectly, exactly how *you* need it to be to keep growing. *Your life is exactly what you need.*

Gratitude reminds me most of The Star card in the tarot. This card (my personal favorite) represents a woman in the moonlight under an open sky of stars; as she is gathering a jug of water from the pond. She has everything she needs and is in the nude. It is a card of everything coming together as planned, a time to relax and be grateful for everything the universe has provided.

Making a gratitude chart/list is easy enough. Think of anything that makes you appreciate being on earth.

Personal Examples

The Angels
Protection
The past, present, and future.
My soul
Spiritual Guidance
Trust

Faith
Existence
Sponsorship
My classes at School

Gratitude Journal/List

I am blessed to be alive and have music in my soul that is positive and full of serenity.

Gratitude Journal Entries (personal)

shoes	tea	breath	life	friends
the ocean	yoga	imagine	the sun	family
arts & crafts	freedom	candles	love	food
beads	happiness	the wind	my body	shelter
seaglass	logic	the sea air	goals	hope

In my journal…

Enjoy Life, Live Well, Happy, and Free. We Love you. - Angels

Love your soul, spirit, and body.

Think good thoughts

good people	water	writing	past	trust
heart	fire	peace	present	spirituality
funerals	music	program	future	existence
weddings	roses	the angels	My soul	wisdom
harmony	appreciate	protection	guidance	empathy

GRATITUDE JOURNAL ENTRY FOR YOU

1. _____
2. _____
3. _____
4. _____
5. _____

5 things

Water
My kitten
Nature
Waterfalls
Candles

I would recommend keeping a gratitude journal and writing in it as often as possible to remind yourself of the beautiful life that is all yours and everything/everyone you appreciate along the way.

blessing ritual

My nieces, my grandmother each wrote down 5 blessings in our lives, then we created a little poem out of the 5 things, which didn't have to rhyme. We each had a candle lit in front of us, then after we finished writing, we said the poems/lists out loud and blew out the candles. It was cute to hear everyone's different values and things that were important to them. Writing or journaling your emotions is such a beautiful thing, and it really helps when you are in a tough spot.

Try it out yourself!

You can do this ritual with a friend, family member, or alone.

Light a candle in front of your piece of paper and pen.

create*

Blessing List (list blessings in your life)

1. _____
2. _____
3. _____
4. _____
5. _____

Now create a poem (or rap) out of your 5 things....

_____

_____

_____

Share or say aloud the list and poem, then blow out your candle.

Imagination RoadMap Meditation

<u>(record saying the meditation then listen)</u>

Imagine you are in a brand new car of your choice and you are following the GPS that the universe installed in your car. Your car can be any color you like. You are going on a trip, but you have no idea where the GPS will take you, how long it will take to get there, or how long you will be staying. In the glovebox is lots of cash enough to buy what you need while you are there. And the universe keeps you safe so you are protected. Now think of someplace that you would absolutely love to visit. Get a feel for it. If you want to close your eyes you can think of how beautiful this place is, and who might be there when you arrive. There is a knowing in your heart that the spirit of the universe has provided a safe journey for you as you are traveling and has even offered a first class train ticket back home. You might be staying in a fancy hotel, a friend's house or family member, or maybe a significant other. Maybe your car is even packed full of people, or maybe you are riding solo. Just know that the universe has taken you this far in life, and the more your fear is channeled into love- the more you will have belief that things will work out. You have a great time on your trip and wonder about all the places you'd love to see without a single worry. You are loved and arrive safely back home where your house plant has missed you.

"Now that she's back in the atmosphere, with drops of Jupiter in her hair........
But tell me, did you sail across the sun?

Did you make it to the Milky Way to see the lights all
faded
And that Heaven is overrated?
Tell me, did you fall for a shooting star?
One without a permanent scar and did you miss me
While you were looking for yourself out there?"------
Drops of Jupiter (Tell Me)- Train

CHAPTER 666

KARMIC CONTRACTS

Karmic Debt
Soulmates vs. Twinflames

(picture)

CHAPTER 666- You may think, wait what? 666 is an angel number? Well in fact, it is.

666 Angel number means to find balance, and don't let negative thinking or fear get to your head.

"Waited long enough that I could never call you-baby how fu*ked is that?"- Shampoo Bottles- Peach Pit

What does having a *karmic contract* mean to anyone? When it comes to intimate relationships the goal is to clean up past life trauma without causing any more baggage or damage. Things do not always go according to your plans or expectations. Universal lessons are *meant* to be challenging. It would be ideal to communicate and understand each other. People get hurt from bad intentions or the things that happen. Other times we create fun times and harmony.

Lessons in Love are Blessings in Life. Protect your Soul.

Questions!!!

Do you believe in soulmates ?

Yes I do believe. I think you can have a soulmate as a friend and soulmate as a partner. I have one, it's hard to explain because you know how you feel. If that person is feeling pain you are in pain because you love them. If you love someone unconditionally that's a sign.

Vanja Spaic

Do you think there is someone meant for everyone in this life?

I actually do think so, they may not end up together but I do think there is someone meant for everyone sometimes people end up alone.

Vanja Spaic

Karmic Relationships, Soulmates, Twinflames, and Life Partners : OH MY!!!

I know everyone wants to talk about **love**. SO- What is the difference between a SOULMATE and a TWINFLAME? A **SOULMATE** is exactly what it sounds like, Someone that you are connected with- someone you have karmic ties too- someone you have a longing for, like when you miss your best friend that you haven't seen in 5 years, but times a million because there is sexual energy involved and *you feel* like you can't help but be emotionally attached, and love them a-lot.Soulmates are *brought together* by the Universe and divine fate. It is the divine law order that they meet again (from past lives) to work on their karmic lessons together so that they learn more and grow together. As soulmates, they have a connection that is long-lasting, deep, strung-out, super lovey dovey, and just harmonious. This might be a person that you could see yourself marrying or you want to be with them forever. There is often a passionate bond and a deep love for one another. More than likely your *life partner* will be one of your soulmates that you meet in life. A **TWIN FLAME**- is more of a high energy type relationship that is best described as a quick, fiery flame that can be put out with the blink of an eye or the lash of one word. You are connected throughout your lifetime. A Twin Flame can be a quick relationship. They often circle back into your life multiple times. It is a super flame of love that is without a doubt intense and a crazy fire. Many say that this is someone you share a soul with, as if your soul was split in half at the time of birth and you have very telepathic type thoughts that are "shared". You can put each other's fire out as easily as it gets started. It is an intense emotional rollercoaster ride that feels like you can't live without each other and you can't even stand each other at other moments. A karmic relationship is a person you cross paths with whom you have unfinished business with that you are meant to resolve in this lifetime. Hopefully you succeed. Technically all relationships are karmic. I'm referring to short-lived experiences with a chance to heal karma from past lives. The chances are whatever kind of romantic or platonic situation this encounter turns out to be, you have either met them in a past life, or only this life because you are a new soul, or an old soul that made a new connection.

Each connection is very different with every soulmate, twin flame or karmic relationship you come across in life. It is a unique energy. Every person will have a different experience because every human has different soul ties. You can have a soul tie with a soulmate or twin flame because the "soul tie" is the energy that keeps pulling you to them. The vibration of LOVE will come up in any relationship. Soulmate energy is long lasting throughout a time period, whereas twin flame energy is sporadic but very intense, and karmic relationship energy is more of a "in the moment" connection because it is meant to be temporary.

When it comes to soulmates, twinflames, and past lives... you can believe what you want. A soul tie connection makes you feel like someone is familiar or feel like you have met them in a previous lifetime. We are designed as SOULS to listen and learn from each other- it's how we stay connected. You can ignore the feelings of being drawn to a certain person- or KNOW for certain you were supposed to be brought together by divine law. Lastly, a *Soul Life Partner* is that one (*the* one) person that you are meant to spend your life with or marry. They can have karmic lives shared, be a twin flame *and* a soulmate. Or just one of those. The point is they are your true love, the person you'll spend the most time with throughout your lifetime. This is someone very long term. It is possible to have multiple life partners.

The new dating world..

When dating, go with your heart and make sure that you're making choices that benefit your well being. How do you know for sure if they are your soulmate OR your twin flame? ASK THE ANGELS/SPIRIT GUIDES (or go with your heart). Use a pendulum, notebook, ask out loud and listen for an answer in meditation, or light a candle and pray about it. On the topic of everything Lovey- Dovey- by now maybe you have dated, been interested in someone, married, divorced, remarried, or even remarried the person you divorced. Maybe you have never dated, had phone sex once, had one night stands, you're a virgin for life, a monk, or a pornstar- I don't know your life! SO!! How do you know, if the person you are with, dating, f*cking, friends with, or just sexting, is your twin flame, soulmate, or karmic relationship? You find out how the energy feels with them. Every romantic encounter you've had matters, and gave you a lesson in love. Every person you have ever come across whether you found each other on facebook messenger, snapchat, instagram, email, or house phone that you have flirted with, hooked up with, dated, facebook stalked, or that catfished you; met *you* for a reason. *whether or not you like them anymore. It doesn't matter if you blocked them, they blocked you, or you wish you never had met them. You have history together because you have past lives together in most cases. You found each other at one point in this lifetime for some forsaken reason we won't speak of, or because *you were meant to find them.*Maybe you are happy about meeting someone special. That's even better because maybe you can get along. The game in 2023 has changed from writing phone numbers down on paper or seeing someone somewhere because you knew where to find them- to swatching digits on cell phones, snapchatting and finding people on dating websites. Making it way too easy for some people to be REAL *fake*. Safety should be the number one priority when it comes to dating. Consent shouldn't be overrated and both partners should be comfortable with what they are doing.

"You can't be a pimp and a prostitute too"- Icky Thump by The White Stripes.

It's important to know you're on the same page with someone you have feelings towards. If you have zero romantic feelings towards someone and are just using them for cash flow- there are more ***creative*** ways to make money than that. Selling underwear on the black market is abnormally normalized. OnlyFans created full time jobs for sex workers and completely risked their livelihood, reputation, and safety. People in the human trafficked system never had a choice. It's become a dangerous war zone out there when it comes to dating, for both men and women. Ordinary people on dating websites are being asked for money by scam artists who convince you they are in love with you. People used to tell eachother how they felt in the form of a letter, in person, calling the house phone and talking for hours, emailing or even myspace. Before cell phones, people just showed up where they thought they would find that person- isn't that a trip? Nowadays that's considered stalking someone. A revolution of technology has begun and we can only get more outlandish from here. No more waiting for your lover's letter by carriage.

"I swear to God on your deathbed you'll think of me, whether I am there or not. "- song lyrics from CRAZY by Jessie Reyes

Love yourself so you can love someone else. You attract the perfect partner that the universe aligns with your unique energy, when the time is right. It happens in divine timing.

Remember that your role in another lover's life also can make a huge impact on them, and how you treat each other will determine the end result of karmic debt for your next lifetime together.

Question time

Do you believe in reincarnation or past lives or not?

I believe in both reincarnation and past lives. I feel we all come from something and we all have a past that's unknown. *-petunia party flower*

Love life lessons are hard and don't always go the way we want them too. You can either reach harmony or return to a negative karmic pattern. *Generational curses* can also get in the way of relationships. This means you carry mistakes your family and you have been making that create similar scenarios repeating throughout generations. It is unique to *your life experience. Your family can have an input and an impact on your romantic love life.*

So, everybody reading this book is in a different scenario regarding LOVE. Maybe you just got out of a relationship, or started a new one. Maybe you are single and loving yourself. These next activities are meant to help you in any experience you might be going through.

"Holding on to anger is like grasping a hot coal with the intent of throwing it at someone else; you are the one who gets burned."- Buddha

If you are caught in the crossfire of a toxic relationship that is now over or ending, you may need some closure. People get deprived of closure in romantic relationships. Miscommunications happen when people don't disclose their true feelings until it's too late. It can be the most frustrating thing to be completely done with someone, and they are unable to receive your ending feelings. Find the closure you need and write them a letter.

Letting Go Letter
Tell them how you feel
On paper...

Letting Go Letter

Think of a romantic partner that you never got closure with or the situation was left unresolved. Maybe you never got the chance to get this off your chest and you think about it all the time- *still*. Guilt or hurt feelings might come up. This can be in divorce or any type of break up. Just write how you feel so that they know once and for all. So that the energy between the two of you can be balanced out. *Just make sure you write everything you never said to them.*

Address your letter to them and from you, but no need to waste a stamp since you aren't sending it. (you can write Looney Toon Land or psycho.com as the address, whatever you want, go nuts!),

I want to remind you this is closure for you! Try to stay sincere about it. :)

Example :

Dear Joe Bob Jr,

Thank you for helping me become a better person. I hope you have a nice life and move on in the most positive way for you.

From,
Katty

Katty
Parkway Drive 567
Bullet for my Valentine,
Columbia

To: Joe Bob Jr.
Love and Light Avenue
Shitshow,Tornado
USA

P.S you can get as personal as you want. We aren't actually sending the letter to your ex boyfriends or girlfriends, unless you want to. Burn the letter in a safe fire pit, or bury it in the earth somewhere away from your space. Also you could dissolve it in water, just don't keep it around. Dispose of it somehow so you don't hang on to any stagnant energy. You don't have to wait for a response, because it's only for your eyes to see anyway. If you want to read it aloud, that's even more powerful. Let the flames ignite a healing for you and that person, so you can be free of negativity or sorrow.

In closing if you would like you can say these words or create something yourself.

THANK YOU
FOR LEAVING MY LIFE
THANK YOU FOR MY LESSONS
BE WELL ON YOUR JOURNEY
YOUR ENERGY IS
LEAVING
MY LIFE
THANK YOU, *goodbye*
~Blessed Be~

> Letting Go Charm
> You'll need :
> A small glass bottle
> 1 bay leaf
> Lavender
> Essential oil (I used Fast Luck)
> Daisy

Write on the bay leaf what resonates with you, like "I love you" on one side and "Goodbye" on the other

Then say or create your own affirmation...

"I let go of the stagnant energy that lingers around my head when I think of you. I allow light and love to enter both of our lives and recreate a space of positive frequency."

So Mote it Be!

Keep with you in your purse or pocket for a reminder that you are letting go.

Did you know that "So mote it be" is a way of closing magical workings? In Freemasonry, it is a way of saying "as Gods will it to be". It was in a Masonic poem called Halliwell Manuscript of Regius Poem- and the saying was reclaimed in neo pagan traditions. Aleister Crowley (who wrote Magic in Theory and Practice (1929)) and Gerald Gardner (father of witchcraft who wrote Witchcraft Today) recycled the phrase in their writings.

CANDLE CORD CUTTING RITUAL with Archangel Michael

Cut ties with any ex-lover altogether-like Harley Quinn did with the Joker.

For this ritual you will need two long candles any size. I used yellow (find happiness) to resemble the other person and purple (third eye: awakening, expanding my mind) for me. So you tie the candles together in a bowl of salt (or cauldron in a safe spot) with some string that is not going to catch your house on fire, like thin hemp rope. Ask Archangel Michael to cut ties with this person. Close your eyes and imagine big silver scissors cutting the cord between you two. Hell, even play some music that reminds you of them. Set an intention for both parties. Then light each candle, and just watch them burn. Pay attention to what happens to each candle, that's _Spirit_ telling you how everything's going down. Some TikTok videos will show one candle falling on the other or melting together. This is to show you what's happening in real life. The point is to let go of the other person and release any toxic feelings leftover. The salt in the bowl is allowing a safe space for each person to energetically calm the F down.

In closing, Thank you Archangel Michael for sending protective energy and cutting away what no longer serves me.

At times we feel sorrow and miss people that once were in our lives- but sometimes they are MEANT to leave our circle.

Here is a quote from the movie 500 days of Summer, a favorite of mine.

Rachel Hansen: Better that you find this out now before you come home and find her in bed with Lars from Norway.

Tom: Who's Lars from Norway?

Rachel Hansen: Just some guy she met at the gym with Brad Pitt's face and Jesus' abs

<u>Cleansing Ritual for Release of Lover</u>

Play music- either something that reminds you of the person, or something that represents how you feel for them now.

Write their name in Red ink on paper and burn in a safe bbq pit or cauldron.

Look at their picture on your phone or regular photo.

Pray for them and release them in good spirits -or just tell them how you feel as if they were listening.

Life is not what we always imagined it might be. The fact is that life changes. Practicing self care and positive affirmations can help your journey in life, which will help you find comfort when you need it most. Life does not always work out perfectly or the way you expected; but just because romantic love doesn't work out; that doesn't mean you should give up. And that means focus on yourself. When your love life fails try not to find the next substitute. Let's face it no one wants to embrace loneliness- but you might feel better without engaging with Mr. or Miss Rebound. Instead take the time you need for yourself and do the things you love. Feeling hurt is natural and a part of life, so be easy on yourself.

QUESTION TIME ********

Have you ever had a broken heart? What did that feel like or how did you heal?

Yes, recently I lost my Aunt, Grandpa, and my uncle, while also being dumped for being "too good of a friend". I have yet to heal, but I use music and reading.

-Phoebe Moore

She paints her eyes as black as night now
She pulls her shades down tight
Girl, give a smile when the pain come
Pain, the only thing don't make it alright

She Talks to Angels by The Black Crowes

Release Bad Breakup Vibes

This is for when little hoodlums keep sending you bad vibes after a bad breakup.

You'll need to light some sage or palo santo and cleanse yourself, then just say this-

All unwanted energy blocking my psychic circle of light is exposed and released now. Thank you for leaving my energy space, I don't need any extra bad vibes in my life. You are released, return to heaven. Go home where you belong. You are welcome to leave the vicinity because my guides are very powerful and are protecting me at all times. All unwanted energy leaves now.

And that is how you ask for the energy to go away. It's obvious when people have evil intentions. Pay attention to this everyday in all encounters.

After the breakups...

When people break up and get divorced, you split the finances, the house, maybe even the kids. You go half and half on the heartache, the memories, the unsolved feelings towards each other- and maybe a little hate or anger. This can also be the result of a breakup with a girlfriend or boyfriend. **No matter what your pronouns happen to be-** it hurts to love someone that doesn't have the same feelings towards you anymore. People have enemies because of what happens in real life, on this earth. Maybe they cheat on you or you cheat on them. Betrayal. Denial. Narcissistic Abuse. Physical Violence. Maybe you have no regrets from your past or current relationship. All I am saying is wherever you are in life, karmic patterns are accumulating as we speak, all around the world. Rape creates even more karmic debt. You know when people say to "pray for your enemies?" It is hard to pray for someone who might have hurt you, but sending them good vibes might just change your whole perspective.

Today is gonna be the day that they're gonna throw it back to you

And by now, you should've somehow realized what you gotta do

I don't believe that anybody feels the way I do about you now

And backbeat, the word is on the street that the fire in your heart is out...

Wonderwall by Oasis

For the people who are trying to find love...

So now that we covered how to get over someone- let's start talking about how to attract the perfect partner that the universe already has in mind for *you*. We're talking about your *soul life partner. This is the person you will likely spend a big chunk of time with once you meet them. They are "the one" you've been waiting to meet your whole life.*

Burning Flame Exercise

This is for anyone that is fully ready for a new life partner.

Think of your ideal partner. Light a candle if you want and make it personal/sacred. Now say aloud:

I AM DESERVING OF A LOVING LIFE PARTNER TO SHARE AND ENJOY MY TIME WITH. I LOVE MYSELF AND I AM READY FOR A NEW ENDEAVOR OF LOVING KINDNESS THAT INVOLVES A NEW RELATIONSHIP. THERE IS A FEELING OF MUTUAL HIGHER CONNECTION WHERE WE ARE IN DEEP BLISS. THANK YOU UNIVERSE FOR ANSWERING MY CLEAR REQUESTS.

Now, take a paper and pen or write on the lines, what your ideal candidate would be like for a soulmate, and try to keep it simple. I wouldn't be specific about the shoe size or color of hair. Just think of the person as someone who already exists on this planet, that is already meant for you. This will help attract them and get the vibes clear. Think of similarities and traits that your ideal partner would have. After that you'll mention any red flags you absolutely couldn't stand for. We ask the Universe to align both of your energies so you can be ready for each other.

My Ideal Life Partner would be like this….

_____

_____

_____

I would not accept these red flags or behaviors….

_____

_____

*outloud

*In Closing, Thank you universe for bringing me a truly loving person in my life who wants to know me for who I am, and who will accept my spirit.

Soul Partner Love Energy Meditation

Get comfortable and
turn on the frequency of love, which is 528 hz, twin flame hertz at 432hz, and 693 hz attracts love. You can find those sounds on YouTube easily.

Soften your eyes, unclench your jaw. Take a few deep breaths. Now for the next few minutes completely relax, and start to imagine being with your soul life partner, enjoying each other's company. Close your eyes and let your mind take you to a place where you are fully absorbed in how fun and harmonious it is to be with your partner. Take a few minutes.

When you open your eyes, keep positive thoughts regarding your soulmate.

Do you think that your soul mate or twin flame is on the same vibe as you?

Think about how your soul partners' vibes match yours for a moment. Do you get a good feeling about them?

Gabrielle Bernstein has a great love meditation album called MediDating: Meditations for Fearless Romance.

A great book that has amazing loving rituals to attract your perfect partner is *The Spiritual Guide to Attracting Love* by Carolyn Boyes.

So you might be asking where can I find my soul life partner? And when will it happen??

Believe it or not I have an answer for you. It's the last place you would think of, and in divine timing. It happens when you least expect it, for real. Let go of all expectations and let the universe work its magic on you.

Let the magick keep happening! Spiritual Singles.com, Kinlia, MeetMindful,and iris are great apps/websites to find a spiritual match. These are places to find a like minded soul on the same wavelength.

Unique cases happen all the time. Love has driven people to do wild, crazy, passionate things! Go with your heart and trust the process. Say *no* to red flags and protect your energy.

Astrology tidbit…

While we are on the topic of relationships, it might be worth exploring astrology. Our astrological birth chart relates to our traits and personalities, *and everyone is very unique.* Think of Western and Vedic astrology as a guideline to understand yourself more as well as the stars and the world. In short, vedic astrology is based off the ever changing phases of planetary alignment, while Western Astrology bases charts off of the "tropical calendar" and the four seasons. Ancient civilizations have studied this for centuries and there is literature and historical symbolism to prove that. People that are born around the same time are often similar.

I'd like to mention Jony Patry, a Vedic Astrologer who teaches vedic astrology courses and makes very accurate world predictions. A few beloved tarot card readers that

I highly recommend and adore that read for each zodiac sign are : Sasha Bonasin and Sarah Vrba. They give you a better understanding of what your main sun sign reflects in the present time. They give accurate weekly or monthly readings for every sign of the zodiac for a collective general reading to prepare you for what is upcoming in your life.

ASTROLOGY QUESTIONS*****

I interviewed a cute young couple that had been together for 6 years who were celebrating her birthday.

What do you think about astrology or your horoscope?

The young guy said: "I feel like it's pretty accurate and I am a Capricorn. Everything about a Capricorn sounds exactly like me."

His Girlfriend is a Virgo and it was her birthday. She resonates with being organized and sarcastic. They believe their relationship will last and that they are compatible.

Virgo and Capricorn, Alyssa and Chris

Anything can happen and it can take a long time to get to know someone. Maybe you can relate. Take your chance when you get the chance to be in love. Try not to hurt others in the process of your search for love.. Find happiness within and let go of the expectations. If you have a partner, they have emotions just like you so keep that in mind. When lovers laugh together, are excited to see each other, have fun and are carefree, there are no worries. Hard times can be a beautiful thing also because you get through things together and learn who they are. Make it easier and simple.

How to keep up with self-care while in a "relation-ship"

Walking
Eating healthy
Meditate
Spend quality time by yourself (reading a book, etc.)
Don't forget about your passions
It's okay to be alone!
If getting some space from them is a healthier option do that!
Talk to a friend, counselor, or family member
Tell yourself that you love you in the mirror
Make sure you're not being sour to your partner or taking shit from them.
Build trust, forgive, let jealousy go
If disagreements/arguments occur- always be respectful
Work on yourselves
Let go of blaming your partner
Address all negative traits

Trigger "Points" for Couples

What is a *trigger* ? It's when something someone said or did made you feel uncomfortable and reminded you of something toxic from your past, or it just doesn't bring you a good feeling at all. Maybe it's antagonizing or inappropriate. Everybody gets triggered, and you need to know how to make your partner feel comfortable. So now you'll list what triggers you; and the negative limited belief that exists. Think of WHY you act the way you do, and have your partner do the same (*if they are willing to*). Think about your romantic history/patterns in relationships in the past. Have you had a tendency to be controlling or jealous? Has you or your partner's insecurity led to self esteem issues or trust issues?

Negative traits can be: Jealousy, Codependency, Egotistical, Controlling, Obsessive, Verbally Abusive, etc. You or your partner might just have a tendency to be one way or the other- try to think of the problems in your relationship and what you both need to work on.

First list anything that your partner says/does that triggers you

Example: My partner brings up my past and judges me.

Then you'll list all the positive traits that you love about your partner. Example: He's constantly making me laugh and smile and we have so much fun together.

Now list the negative limited beliefs that you know you are guilty of or your partner...

Example: I check his phone because I am insecure that he doesn't love me.

_____

_____

Now rewrite the negative belief as a positive affirmation.

Example: My partner loves me and reassures me that I am exactly what he needs in his life.

_____

_____

If you did this exercise as a couple: now you will discuss the triggers and negative limited beliefs and more importantly take the positive affirmations and put them on the wall so you can repeat them aloud. You can toss the negative beliefs or burn them. You can take a piece of paper and write multiple issues if you want. Just make sure that each person says the affirmation out loud after you create it. When you notice that anyone starts going back to old behaviors, *address it right away* with each other. Communication is a love medicine, we all need it very often.

"I've been seein that red corolla parked out on the corner there, if it was yours it'd be some hippie bullshit hanging from the rearview mirror" - Shampoo Bottles by Peach Pit

<u>*Written by Kat!*</u> *: My damn happily ever after is a hippie wedding in the sand or the forest with beautiful jewels and real flowers and party favors that I handmade. And some spiritual guy waiting to kiss me with open arms and the indefinite love which he explains in the vows. I am talking about 3 kids, traveling the world, and staying together for a fun and beautiful relationship, which leads us to our deathbeds of a viking ceremony where*

our children are crying because they love us so much and each handcrafted a goodbye letter from the heart. I am talking about all that glitters is gold and all that is silver we can hold.

If someone is beautiful and you want to tell them that and it's on your heart- Why go against nature? Humans feel nice about compliments. I think we all feel nice when people are nice to us. Everyone is truly BEAUTIFUL. When we love and appreciate each other the world is a better place. *Attraction starts getting hotter when the emotional connection is on point. #truth*

"You cut out a piece of me..so there you go, can't make a wife out of a hoe." - The Kid LAROI

She don't know no lover
None that I've ever seen
To her that don't mean nothin'
But to me, it means
Means everything
-She Talks to Angels by The Black Crowes

I love myself so f*cking much I'm so proud of me ! I did it!! <3 loving myself FOREVER and EVER!!

CHAPTER 777

RECOVERY FROM ADDICTION, MENTAL HEALTH, AND CODEPENDENT VIBES

Numbers 777: These angel numbers are associated with luck, prosperity and divine guidance.

She never mentions the word "addiction"
In certain company
Yeah, she'll tell you she's an orphan
After you meet her family

She Talks to Angels by The Black Crowes

"I am not my body. The Mind is my servant. I keep my eyes on the divine. " - SRI & KIRA

"We have found much of Heaven and we have rocketed into the fourth dimension of existence of which we had not even dreamed." -Alcoholics Anonymous

Questions

<u>*What is it like to have hope or what is it like to be hopeless?*</u>

"I imagine hope as being able to know there is a tomorrow. It seems dark today, but it will get better. Be it the Stars, God, or something else. Hopeless would be the opposite of that. I was homeless in Oceano, I lost my mom to cancer, and had tried to commit suicide. My brother saved my life and cut the rope. The light at the end of the tunnel was my mom. Hopeless is no light at the end of the tunnel." - *Nala Nelson*

Website for international suicide prevention- <u>https:// findahelpline.com</u>

"Please amplify the feeling of faith and hope within my heart. Remind me that I am on a journey and this experience is all

part of the divine plan. So be it, so it is." -from the definition of "hopelessness" in the book DEAR UNIVERSE by Sarah Prout

There are resources, spiritual principals, counselors, doctors, and facilities dedicated to helping people struggling with health problems because of their addiction or even who have thoughts of suicide. If you or someone you know needs help please call the suicide hotline and they will help you. <u>When you feel helpless, hopeless, struggling and upset-know there is always someone to listen to you. Relax and calm down. Think about the people in your life that love you and the people that you love.</u>You don't want to miss out on spending quality time with your soul family, believe me! I know what it feels like to not have happy feelings towards yourself and experience an in depth sadness in your soul. But the light will prevail. You can make it. I guarantee the universe wants you alive to experience the vibration of love right at this instance. *Knowing that someone else truly cares could stop you from missing out on life.* People come from many different walks of life and there is someone out there that really does know how you feel, whether they are walking or in a wheelchair! Anything can happen so cherish the people around you while you have them. If you give in, you may see what the bright future holds ahead.

Caption: this kitty is loving the NA program. (Hehe)*I went to an NA meeting in Mexico and they were welcoming and kind to me. I had walked a few miles to get there and was so happy to find home.Even though I don't speak spanish, the language of the heart is universal.

My personal recovery journey... *(from hopeless dope to hopeful dork)(lol)*

In 2013, I came back from a music festival and had taken a large amount of MDMA. Having a drug induced psychosis changed my life. Hearing voices, having hallucinations, ongoing internal dialogue, conversations with myself, crying spells everyday for years- those were just a few side effects of what happened. I have been through rehab, Mental Institutions, Outpatient Dual Diagnosis programs, have gone to Alcoholics Anonymous, Narcotics Anonymous, and Refuge Recovery. I have lost my mind trying to find myself. My experience has been that the longer you are sober, the better you feel. Narcotics Anonymous and Alcoholics Anonymous helped save my life because they gave me the tools to stay grateful and know that other people go through the same thing. Recovery made me aware that making amends can make a difference, I can love myself, forgive others and let things go. Feeling all your emotions and pain without using an unhealthy habit to replace that feeling is challenging, but f*cking beautiful and raw! There really are long term effects after using drugs to your brain. My family supported me. In Costa Mesa, CA, I received a brain scan (MRI), at one of Dr.Amen's clinics. Dr. Amen and his wife are amazing mental health advocates, and he has a Ted Talk with his personal story. When I received my appointment with the psychiatrist at the clinic, she showed me a picture of my scan. She was so cute the way she explained things to me. She said all the red spots on my brain were damaged (from drug use), and that my brain was lit up like a christmas tree! She also said that the areas affected would alter my mood, sleep, and emotions. Which sounds about what I go through on a daily basis.

One fun night out can literally change everything. I could beat myself up about it, but I choose to forgive myself and move on. Deal with the cards that life gives you and keep going. Never look back. I am proof that it's a little tough to get back on your feet. Recovery meetings have helped me to get clarity in my mind and hear other people talk from a different perspective on what works for them. Recovery programs are for people with substance abuse problems, mental illness, or any form of addiction. If you suffer from drug or alcohol addiction and mental illness, that is called Dual Diagnosis. I went to the Cottage Hospital in San Luis Obispo, CA for a Dual Diagnosis program that had meditation groups and family meetings. It was a place to talk about your mental health in an open space. I hold Cottage dear to my heart because it is the same hospital branch where my Grandpa attended an alcoholic treatment center many years ago. Having a drug-induced psychosis is part of my story, and it complicated my life. Screaming in my car, disrespecting people, having zero patience, experiencing hypomania, being an emotional wreck, those are normal reactions after going through something like this. *And I am not alone. Many of us struggle.* Over the years, from learning from others it has forced me to practice kindness, start being aware of how I treat people, enjoy small things in life and force myself to relax and breathe instead of fidgeting and going through life like a pacing maniac. *I swear to you it gets better. Time heals EVERYTHING! Life is amazing.* Practicing self-discipline and changing who I am over and over to become a better person. *I am literally so proud of myself for making it this far because I know where I have been. There were times I laid on the floor crying wishing for my life to end, begging the angels to please take me away. For some reason they kept me around, wink wink.*

Luckily,western medicine had a pretty big role in *my personal* recovery journey. It has just been a no brainer. Every doctor that has ever helped me out is literally an Angel from Heaven. I would have been a dangerous person without it, especially in the very beginning after the event. Staying sober, finding spirituality, and self help methods helped me grow as a person. I have finally learned how to act like an adult (most of the time lol) while staying a kid at heart, and re-learned how to be a normal member of society. I can't tell you how grateful I am for my counselors that validated my feelings and made me feel worthy of starting over. Some of my family members didn't understand it or know what to do, and *some of them* will never get it. Some of them put all judgements aside and fully accept me, and try to understand and support me. I had to find my own support groups and be independent. Being sober made me think about all the other addictions I have engaged in over the years of my life. I have struggled with gambling, bulimia, being in debt, binge drinking, smoking weed, experimenting with other drugs, having too many sex partners, overeating, shopping, addicted to relationships, codependency, and hoarding.

There have been times where I have felt so alone in this universe. But seeing that people actually care about me just enough to pass a kleenex box, give me a hug, or help me to calm down after a break down, gives me hope. There have been times in my life full of anxiety and tears, where I was praying and hoping that no one would talk to me. That I could be left alone to be hopeless. But people do care and they are nice if you give them a chance. When I meet people like that it really makes me want to live longer.

Affirmation: *I love to spend time with people in my life that f*cking deserve my energy and accept me 100% as I am **right now.***

<u>Addiction to Drugs and Alcohol</u>

NA JUST FOR TODAY reading: "A clean addict, is indeed, a vision of hope."

Great Recovery Books: Recovery 2.0 by Tommy Rosen, Rewired by Erica Spiegelman, Codependent No More by Melody Beattie, Refuge Recovery by Noah Levine.

The new gateway drug to a better future is a clear spiritual awakening. It's appealing, it's attractive, and we can see how far people get in life and the great rewards when people stay sober. Jeopardizing your brain health with drugs and alcohol is risky. Everybody is dealt different cards in life. Some people might not even notice when you get sober. Prove to yourself and everyone that your change is for the better. Stay positive always. And just relapse as many times as you f*cking have to without dying. It's unrealistic to think people won't f*ck up every once in a while. Everyone is perfect as you are!!! You are amazing and you are doing so great.. keep going!!!

"You can check out anytime you like, but you can never leave" "Some dance to remember, some dance to forget"- Hotel California -The Eagles

There are a few things that stick out to me from those recovery programs. "There is a solution." "One day, one minute, one second at a time." "Just for today"

The resources available for AA and NA meetings are accessible anywhere around the world. The two apps that are helpful to find a meeting are Meeting Guide for AA and the Narcotics Anonymous app. You can also look for the official website of the type of meeting you need for the county you live in. There are even dating apps for people in sobriety, there are conventions with concerts and rap battles, with meetings all night long. I went to an A.A convention in L.A with a friend, and there was a punk show and dance for half the night. Now that zoom is so popular, you can also find meetings online that have people from all around the world! If you get the opportunity to be of service, that might help you to stay responsible. I am stressing this information because altering your mind creates unmanageable psychosis. Forgive yourself, let go and surrender to the universe. It's hard for everyone to stop worrying about the mistakes we have made, that is natural because we have a conscience. According to Oxford Languages- a conscience is an inner feeling or voice viewed as acting as a guide to the rightness or wrongness of one's behavior.

Just don't let the past eat you up. Move on and forgive yourself. Own that shit and let go of it.

NA World Service Telephone- 1-818-773-9999
AA WORLD SERVICES- 1-212-870-3400

If you struggle with Marijuana Addiction, there are meetings for that. There is scientific evidence that marijuana triggers psychosis with long term use.

MA (Marijuana Anonymous) World Services- 800-766-6779 Get hooked up with the right meetings that could change your way of thinking. Be safe out there.

Drug Abuse National Hotline- 800-662-4357
Cocaine Hotline (24 hours)- 1-800-262-2463
Ecstasy Addiction- 1-800-468-6933

If 12 step meetings turn you off, there are different options for recovery meetings. One is called Refuge Recovery. These are meditation-recovery meetings based off of buddhist principles that are very open-minded and easy to follow. It started in Santa Cruz when Noah Levine wrote the book Refuge Recovery. He started the Against the Stream Meditation Center which is in Venice Beach, CA.

The Three Principles Global Community promotes 3 principles, which are The Universal Mind, Thought, and Consciousness. The book they go by is The Serenity Principle by Joseph V. Bailey.

SOBRIETY IS AWESOME

The Serenity Prayer, The Big Book of A.A, (altered by me)

"Spirit of the Universe, Grant me the Serenity to accept the things I can change, the courage to change the things I can, and the wisdom to know the difference."

The easy 12 steps...

Start working on yourself and growing as a person

Realize other people can help you and the spirit of the universe is always with you

Believe whatever the frack you want

Realize you might have made some mistakes and try to do better, love yourself for where you are *now*

Write down what you think will help you on your personal journey in life and what your going to do about it

Let Karma work it's magic on you

Surround yourself with high vibe people and trust that the universe has your back

If people are affected by your addiction or codependency, think about if you want them in your life. If you do, will it be a struggle or is it possible to make amends? Does anyone need to make amends to you?

Do the thing that makes you feel good (the right thing) ALL THE TIME, whenever possible, also practice telling the truth

Keep paying attention to the way you treat people and how they treat you. Does that feel right?

Meditate and talk to spirit or just keep talking to yourself- know that all the answers are already within, within a book, within another person/angel/daemon, or the universe itself, the point is you can find the answers somewhere around here

Try your best and spread the word of enlightenment to all beings, be a good person

In the Daily Reflections book for Alcoholics Anonymous, March 2nd reading is on HOPE and in Page 60

"Do not be discouraged." In this reading it also says "Hope is the key that unlocks the door of discouragement."

Back to your story...

It might feel like "the war on drugs" is the story of your life, but please hang on dear one. No one wants to see another overdose or death, no one wants you to die. There is an answer! And that answer is to be true to yourself because you are the one that knows if you have a problem, regardless of your drug of choice.

After AA meetings, the party starts and it's a cigarette bumming carnival. But did I mention that you can save at least 30 bucks a week just by quitting smoking cigarettes? If you are struggling with quitting smoking cigs, **Health Vape** is a pretty cool alternative to cigarettes. Put an end to the headaches, bad breath, gum disease, and lung cancer. Health Vape has great flavored vitamin inhalers/pens that are all natural with no nicotine The vitamins target an energizing mood, relaxing feeling, or immunity with great stuff like vitamin c, melatonin, collagen or B12. It is non addictive and made to be "puffed" around 3 times a day rather than 400 (lol).

Taking Mullein can clear out mucus from your lungs from any toxic damage that has taken place.

Codependency

We care so much about others that at times it can be overbearing and overwhelming to the addict (whatever they are addicted to) suffering! Try to let go. Forgive them. Move on from the past and don't guilt trip them for it. Try to support people with whatever they want to do! I know it's hard but let them spread their wings like a butterfly and roam! Let people do what they want. If they ask for your advice, give them your best input without forcing them to make a decision that you want them to. Let them be who they are. Everyone finds a way to do that anyways. Might as well let people do what they wanna do and believe whatever they want. YOLO! Make your time with them count, and make it fun!

When the drugs aren't all that you're addicted to and "everything in moderation" becomes a joke..

So, someone once said to me that it's not all ice cream and orgasms. I think we can all agree those two things are amazing and you always want more. And you can find ways to have what you desire. When is it enough? When do you abuse the power and your hand goes numb or broken and you've gained 20 pounds from eating ice cream everyday? There has to be some kind of balance. My point is, every crack addict likes to get high. But is that buzz, worth every cent of your child's college fund, or even the box of cheerios that they need for dinner tomorrow? Frack no, and that's when addiction takes over your livelihood.

Easy Enough

Coming back to the topic of orgasms real quick. Track your ovulation, use condoms or neem oil for protection, and be free to explore your sex shop options. If you can get your hands on eco friendly and body safe products that's even better. It's important to honor the energy exchange with any partner. Kundalini yoga and clearing your chakras will really help to achieve the most liberating high energy sexual experience. If you and your partner can be open with communication and understand each other emotionally, and get along in a healthy manner, the bedroom will be legit. Leaving guilt and shame behind- there is

more room for flipping pleasure. And speaking of flipping out- understanding how to pleasure each other is a divine masculine and divine feminine experience- when the sexes are balanced and can find healthy ways to channel anger- your relationships will literally amaze you.

If you think you have a problem and need guidance, test out a meeting just to see what it's like. It might be a wake up call. Take everything with a grain of salt. Haha.

Sex Addicts Anonymous (SAA)- https://saa-recovery.org/ 800-477-8191

ON THE HOTLINE...

These Hotlines are Anonymous and Confidential, so don't be afraid to ask for help! It is great to have someone to talk to that is outside of your circle that might understand better than you think!

GA (Gamblers Anonymous)-626-960-3500
OA (Overeaters Anonymous) (available in 20 countries) -https://oa.org
(Just one more Chip, said Lays) Sure, Sure one more chip.
Eating Disorder Awareness and Prevention- 1-800-931-2237
National Association of Anorexia Nervosa and Associated Disorders- 1-847-831-3438

There are resources like free counseling or facilitated groups for people that have experienced sexual assault or domestic violence. There is help for any unique situation and Safe Havens that create a supportive environment for victims. It just takes a bit of research to find these places.

National Sexual Assault Hotline- 1-800-656-HOPE(4673)
Dating Abuse and Domestic Violence
Loveisrespect (24/7)- 1-866-331-9474
National Domestic Violence Hotline- 1-800-799-SAFE
Battered Women and their Children- 1-800-252-8966
Rape, Abuse, and INCEST National Network- RAINN- the nation's largest anti-sexual violence organization:

1-800-656-4673
Do not be afraid to get the help you need.

The **Mary Kay Ash Foundation** is a nonprofit that funds domestic violence shelters like the local one in Fresno, **The Marjaree Mason Center**, changing womens' lives. They also fund cancer research specific to cancers affecting women. Mary Kay Ash inspired many women to become successful in creating their own businesses and keep living her legacy of feminine independence.

Down with My Demons Podcast by Chloe Lionheart has a wonderful episode about giving consent in relation to sex. It's called Sex Series: A "Not so Black and White" Conversation about Consent. Would highly recommend listening to this, it covers a lot of information and a lovely yogi psychotherapist Lisa Chatham is interviewed who has great input.

Thank Buddha, a revolution of equality seems to be spreading like a wildfire of contagious disease. Not everywhere in the world is a safe place where everyone has rights! If these elites supported and accepted everyone, we'd be living in a different universe!

Rainbow Universal

Black Lives Matter. Women's Rights Matter. LGBTQ/ Transgender rights matter. We all f*cking matter right? HUMAN RIGHTS MEANS ALL HUMANS. Whatever ethnicity, gender, or religion you are, we should all be treating each other as equals. LGBTQ rights are valid and all humans belong on this planet. I believe in equality, interracial marriages, and transgender rights. I believe in gay/lesbian rights, being open in sexuality and being free to express yourself with clothing and style. Everyone has a different shape, skin color, eye color, genitalia, hair whether it's curly or straight or long or short, even different colored toenails. What it comes down to is loving people for who they are. Embrace who you are and your f*cking identity that you create. Embrace and accept each other. Genitals are removed in some countries AS TRADITION *WITHOUT THE INDIVIDUALS CHOICE*. Slavery is still alive in the world. Abuse is world wide on a psychological and physical level. Pray for healing in this f*cking universe, because we need it. Some people have to use plastic surgery because it could *save their life. Let's love ourselves a little deeper than the surface for once. Be grateful for another day on earth. Heal from Trauma in your body and your chakras. Ask for healing.* You are perfect as you are. Accept people for who they are. Accept yourself as you are while you are at it. Basically, who cares what people think. *Just Be You. Self. We all have divine feminine energy and divine masculine energy. Take the societal labels out of it and become whatever you want, whoever you want to be.*

Homelessness

People need help that are suffering physically, mentally, and emotionally, who are part of our soul family. People have to take care of each other. There are homeless coalitions, shelters, and housing available in some places. There are nonprofits that are helping out and government programs that are helping them. But the overwhelming numbers of people in America that are homeless or soon to be homeless just keeps getting larger. They need MORE help. The societal wages and the living expenses are not even close to manageable and so many Americans are struggling financially. The communities are hanging by a thread of corruption. As a society we gotta start picking up the pieces and really change some lives instead of staring out the window feeling guilty and helpless. *We* are trying. *We got this. We love each other. Frack the system. We want change. I am personally forming a nonprofit to help the homeless, stay tuned.*

A forty ounce to freedom is the only chance I have to feel good
Even though I feel bad
And I know that, oh, I'm not goin' back
Oh not going back
Oh God knows I'm not going back
-40 oz to Freedom by Bradley Nowell (Sublime)
Rest in Peace Beautiful Soul!

Mental Health

We all go through different things in life. Some people might have anxiety or insomnia. Bipolar Disorder or ADHD. It's a struggle. Each day remember how lucky you are to be alive and to have the energy to keep moving forward! You got this! *Keep going and surround yourself with positive, supportive people.*

The National Alliance on Mental Illness (NAMI) helpline - 800-950-6264

Is a resource for people with a mental illness. Get connected with other individuals nationwide that understand you.

www.pleaselive.org
International Bipolar Association Crisis Line- 1-800-273-TALK(8255)

This is 24/7 availability and free.

Getting a professionals' opinion on your life is a big plus. Counseling has been a lifesaver for me personally. It may seem like ugh, why do I have to tell a total stranger all my problems? That outsiders' perspective might just save your life. And you don't have to admit that you are the problem in your life, they might just have some beneficial tools to help you on your journey to getting well. We all want to be well, they are just trying to help. A few sites for counseling from Licensed Psychologists are TalkSpace and Betterhelp.

A few apps that will help your mental health- Calm, Happify, Headspace, Moodfit, MoodMission, MindBliss, notOK, What's Up?, Moodkit, I am Sober, Quit That, IMoodjournal, eMoods, Recovery Record, Rise up and Recover, Lifesum,NOCD, Worry Watch, Rootd, PTSD Coach,Breathe2Relax, Schizophrenia HealthStorylines, Ten Percent Happier.

There is an answer! And that answer is to be true to yourself.

Dual Diagnosis and Brain Health

Taking brain supplements like fish oil helps heal your brain. There are also contraindications for certain herbs and psych meds so check online for drug interactions. Everyone taking herbal supplements will have a different reaction, so it's best to try what works for you. Sam-e and St. John's wort can be an interaction with bipolar disorder and is not safe to take with SSRI'S (antidepressants). Good brain supplements to take if you are recovering from severe drug induced psychosis would be fish oil, gaba, NAC, or ginseng. I also personally like Ginkgo Bilbao for increased memory function. Give your brain time to heal. What to also avoid if you are on psych meds : excessive caffeine or any supplements that will increase your heart rate too much. Weight loss supplements such as garcinia cambogia or green tea extract increase heart rate and could cause palpitations for people taking medicine. You don't want to create extra symptoms besides all the other ones you have to deal with when you are taking medications. Common side effects from psych meds are heart problems, nausea, headaches, hand or body tremors, constipation, excessive drowsiness, mania, psychosis symptoms such as hallucinations or hearing voices, heart palpitations, hives, and more. So if you have to take medications for mental illness that was caused by an illegal drug use, be prepared for a long healing journey. Always research symptoms and talk to your doctors to make the changes that you need. *TIME* HEALS YOUR BRAIN!!!!

Mental health awareness helps us recognize how stress on the body, mind, and spirit affects us on a daily basis whether we want it to or not. Find an outlet or just be. It's ok to feel your feelings.

"I'm on the wrong side of heaven and the righteous side of hell." - Wrong Side of Heaven by Five Finger Death Punch

Be there for others..

When you are looking at someone and they are sharing stuff that is personal and they are confining in you to not be judged, just listen. You don't have to know all the answers. Hear their story and let them know what they truly need to hear,without selfish input. Try not to be judgemental. It is easier said than done. How many times have you told someone a crazy plan you have to go through with, they tell you not to do it, then you walk away feeling like shit and knowing you are not going to listen to them? Tell *your soul family* your personal information, not outsiders. It's best to go with your instinct, and when you are listening to someone just be supportive in some way. Even if you don't agree with someone's actions, you can still be respectful and opinionated at the same time. *Shame and Blame is not the way to go. Let them tell you whatever they want to do and let spirit give you the words they need to hear.*

Creating a Self-Love Box (instead of a secret stash)

Take a pretty box or any box and write Self Love or Self Care on the outside. Make this a box that has a few of your favorite things that relate to caring for yourself. Some examples to have in your box are essential oils, (i like peppermint for headaches), an eye pillow, headphones, a journal, sage, a few dollars (just in case), or immunity vitamins. You can make it unique and tape your picture on the inside or draw on it. Write a nice note to yourself that you can read later in a time where you really need some support. Affirmations are also a great thing to include in the box. Little things that are meaningful.You could put anything in your self- love box that speaks to you, it's just a reminder to take a moment to do something for you, all found in one place. For instance, don't put a candy wrapper that will attract ants or a used condom.

Litter Bug Anonymous- 1-800-(buy a Lasso Loop)

I once saw a video on Ridiculousness (I made my grandma watch it), where a guy throws trash out of the car window and a guy walking opens his car door and kicks him. Take care of Mother Earth because she could take you out via black hole in outer space if she wanted to. We only get one environment on earth for so many generations to come, take care of this planet so our kids can live in peace! Humans and animals will be healthier and happier with a cleaner planet!! We got this!

Extra Hotlines just in case (for America)

Child Abuse National Hotline- 1-800-25ABUSE
United States Elder Abuse Hotline- 1-866-363-4276
Children in Immediate Danger- 1-800-the-LOST
Missing Children Help Center- 1-800-872-5437
American Cancer Society- 1-800-227-2345
Elder Care Locator- 1-800-422-6237
Teen Hope Line- 1-800-394-HOPE
United Way Crisis Helpline- 1-800-233-HELP
Family Violence Prevention Center- 1-800-313-1310

GriefShare- 1-800-395-5755
Trevor Hotline (suicide)- 1-866-4-U-TREVOR
United States Missing Children Hotline- 1-800-235-3535
Poison Control- 1-800-942-5969
National Runaway Switchboard 1-800-621-4000
Youth Crisis Hotline-1-800-448-4663
S.A.F.E(Self Abuse Finally Ends) 1-800-DONT-CUT

Did something happen at work you don't feel comfortable reporting to HR? This website www.ALLVOICES.com for any kind of harassment, bullying, Culture issues, Bias, General Feedback, and other concerns. Submit a report to the Website.

General CRISIS 24/7- TEXT- SUPPORT to 741-741
Veterans Crisis Line- Veterans Association 24/7: 1-800-273-8255

Chances are someone is out there willing to help you and calm you down.

If you struggle with addiction of any kind or someone that you love is struggling, the first step is to reach out and get the help that you need. THERE IS HOPE and YOU CAN DO THIS!! Hang on for dear life!

STAY WELL <3

"I simply had to believe in a Spirit of the Universe, who knew neither time nor limitation."- Book of A.A

Speaking of Hope, a yummy hummus company called HOPE has totally organic and clean ingredients. HopeFoods actually has a "Spread Hope" page that includes amazing self care activities, mental health assistance, breathwork and decreasing anxiety, tips on exercise, connecting with others, and having gratitude. It's a website worth checking out, and by the way their hummus is to die for- not literally- wink wink. I don't think you can overdose on hummus, but you can overdose on Hope, which makes us all a bunch of dreamers.

Website:

https://hopefoods.com/havehope/

Let your light guide you home.

CHAPTER 888

THE NARCISSIST/THE EMPATH/ EGO VS. COMPASSION

<u>Number 888 means karma. What goes around comes back around.</u>

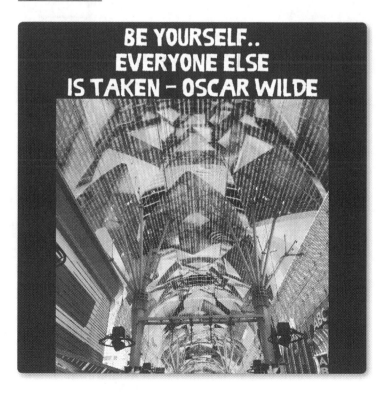

Relationships take Effort.

Engaging in negative destructive self-talk, or Screaming and cursing might temporarily make you feel better, but what you say outloud has such a huge impact on your relationship with yourself. We carry our vibes into the workplace, family environment, or at a friends' party. Harmonize the love for yourself and everything will fall into place. When you tell yourself that you _love yourself_ and speak beautiful words towards yourself or in the mirror, you give yourself a chance to truly evolve and heal. Change your words to a kind, empathetic language so you are speaking to your heart directly and building a comfortable relationship with yourself.

Death of your Ego…

"I have the dream again, I have the dream again
My ego dies at the end, it's ego death
I live the dream like I still don't know what it meant
Who am I? I've lost the thread

My ego dies at the end" - Jensen McRae

*****Questions*****

Do you ever feel like people judge you based on your clothes, religion, tattoos, or any type of beliefs?

I definitely believe most people have judgment towards outward appearance. Certain Generations are different. Most people are *programmed to judge appearance but most stereotypes aren't truthful.*

Holographic Beauty

Limited thinking is toxic judgments on others, gossip, destruction, chaos, and negativity that stems from narcissistic traits and behaviors, or negative toxic beliefs such as self esteem or self loathing.

When you start shedding old patterns and things you have always believed to be true or the right way of thinking that are just not "high vibe"; you will create new, uplifting, nice ways to talk to yourself and treat others.

"All human actions are motivated at their deepest level by two emotions-fear or love."- Conversations with God by Neale Donald Walsch. Neal Walsch asks very open questions to god in his books and he allows the pen and paper to work a bunch of magic. He allows "god" to answer his questions fluently. He basically openly shared his relationship with his higher power which I think is very brave.

Our thoughts are coming from either our brain or our heart. Feelings, thoughts, and emotions come from both.

The Greek mythology story of *Narcissus* goes like this :a young man had many admirers that were nymphs and youths that seeked out his love, but he turned them away in a *nonchalant careless* manner. In each version of the story he refuses different admirers who end up wanting revenge or to teach him a lesson. In one version Ameinias, a young man, falls in love with Narcissus, and Narcissus pays no attention to him. The nymph then commits suicide at his doorstep. Nemesis, the goddess of revenge, lured Narcissus to the Styx river when he was very thirsty after hunting, and he fell in love with his own reflection in the water. He becomes distracted and obsessed with his image- falling in love with his reflection. In some versions of the story he cannot have his object of desire so he gazes into the river for so long that he dies at the river, in other versions he drowns or commits suicide. His body disappears and he transforms into a white and gold flower, still known today as the Narcissus flower.

Modern Day Selfishness

Narcissism is a well known trait/diagnosis known as a personality disorder nowadays. It is about negativity, insecurities, and inability to have empathy. Narcissism let's people walk right over your boundaries, and purposely trigger you or gossip because of jealousy. It makes life much more complicated and often superficiality is used as a tactic. Everyone has an ego, and everyone engages in some level of selfishness, it is only human nature. Being an empath is a healthy way to embrace that ego, every part of yourself and always practice kindness. Empaths have been traumatized by narcissism and that is why they are the strongest people that keep moving forward even when people around them are just plain awful. We get narcissistic traits when people hurt us. We get selfish, thinking if we hurt them back they will stop traumatizing. But they have trauma that needs healing to begin with, that they likely have never faced. So that pain is trapped somewhere around the level of self esteem. Working on your shadow side can help realize what you need to work on as an individual. That means embracing change. Most people with narcissistic qualities have trouble finding acceptance of themselves or others, blame others for problems out of nowhere, and constantly are in denial. In a harsh way, Narcissism is a miserable hell, dragging everyone around into a snowball of pathetic reality. *Fighting, name calling, and nasty low blows is not communication.*

It's a negative cycle, but the only way out is to truly practice self love.

Here's the good news! You can identify your traits and change that sh*t! Narcissism can be reversed, treated, and healing will help to grow as a person! Embrace the Narcissist in you, and love yourself so much that you naturally exude confidence. Take that energy to other people and compliment them, bring eachother up!! For reals find something you love about someone's outfit and comment on it. Make each other feel amazing, so we can all love each other deeper!!!

There's lots of information out there now about Narcissism and Empaths. Dr. Ramani is a great psychologist that has a YouTube channel full of freaking awesome information about how to understand narcissism and how empaths can cope when dealing with people that are close to them who think everyone else is the problem and never seek help. Narcissistic people will often project and put the attention on you, saying that you are the one who needs therapy or help. They may have experienced some sort of trauma that was never addressed, leaving a void. They will say counseling is for people that need it, not them. A lot of narcissists are afraid of therapy or don't think they need it, but therapy is an amazing tool that can change your whole life. Talking through your feelings and actively listening to the activities the psychologist/therapist recommends, really can make a huge impact on you.

It will give you some basic self help tools that everyone can benefit from.

Therapy, Google, and books are great ways to learn more about psychology,using affirmations, meditation, or journaling are great techniques to dive into self exploration. This can only benefit you and those around you. Other methods include exercise, getting a kitten, yoga, saying kind words to yourself, getting out into nature, or less screen time.

*It's difficult to achieve harmony if you have family members, close friends, coworkers, or romantic partners in your life that have narcissistic traits and behaviors or use abusive tactics to manipulate and belittle you.*Engaging in judging others and having negative reactions create harmful intentions. When people use sexist or racist tactics they separate themselves from others. They judge your actions and anything they can use against you which can drive a person mad. Negative intentions come into play often in a subconscious-like manner. Fear of change can create more insecurities. Which is all exhausting for people around narcissism, especially empaths. Hurting other people or attempting to, all in hopes to get a reaction creates guilt and shame. This will eventually eat at the narcissist and it will be a double edged sword that only hurts themselves in the end. This is guilt and shame, imagine living with those feelings constantly. Does that sound very fun? That's why people practice telling the truth. Narcissistic tactics along with verbal abuse, all root from insecurities caused by: <u>FEAR</u>. When they refuse to see their own faults in things but constantly blame you or negatively criticize you, it can get old very fast: and last I hear no one seems to be getting any younger. The good news is all these negative behaviors can definitely be changed and loving yourself, growing as a person, and showing compassion is the most attractive thing you can do as a human! Anotherwards life is short**, make it count!**

#HighVibeSoulFam

Chair Exercise

My counselor (lol) told me about a great method to release feelings. If there is anyone you can't talk to without arguing or someone you probably will never see again… this is the perfect exercise for you. You will pull up a chair and imagine they are sitting in it. Say everything you want to say to that chair, as if that person was really listening. Get it off your chest. Do it while no one is home or in a secluded place for your privacy. Say everything you need to say like they are really there. You'll feel better. You might cry. I did. It works like bloody hell.

It really works if you just let yourself be vulnerable and pretend they are listening to you!

Closure Prayer

When you don't seem to be getting any closure from your expired relationship or your boss that fired you, or maybe even that mean person that ghosted you- try this.

Say aloud

"Since you refuse to end things with me- I will end things with you. The energy we have exchanged is exhausting/ draining. Please let me go. Open your heart to forgiveness and moving on. I want only light energy to surround your presence, and I ask the angels to protect my aura and my energy as I let go of the past. Thank you for being a blessing and lesson in my life. I continue learning and growing. I hope you do the same and truly find the best ways to live your life in the most healthy, meaningful manner. Thank you."

All the talk about Positive Self-Talk, being Empathic, and self love talk

Empaths or "light workers" are born into a world of darkness. They bring the vibration up wherever they go, and they have a whole lot of unconditional love that they choose to share. Empaths feel other people's energies frequently and are able to decipher between someone that feeds off negativity (energy vampires) and someone that just has a pure heart. What I want to remind you is that every person is actually still human. But that being said; it's still your life and the type of people you attract is kind of the vibes you're going through. Sometimes people with lower vibes are attracted to you because they have lessons to learn from you; whether they do is not up to you. And even if you have a lot to learn, that is something to be open to! Have you ever been around someone that is so high energy that you love it? It feels good right? We all go through phases and cycles just like the moon. Your soul family is the family you choose to be around that vibe with you. Then there are biological family members who you are either born around, or find later. No matter what has occurred, you made this choice to be born and chose this path, whether you want to accept that or not. No matter how terrible the upbringing or maybe how loving and beautiful that childhood was for you; it gives you the strength and resilience to be a better human today.

Drum roll.....Questions!!!

Tell me what you think the difference is between Love and Fear..

Love does not cause "butterflies"/anxiety, love leaves people feeling at ease while fear causes the butterfly feeling." - Phoebe Moore

I am home where the waves meet the sand.

The Heart

Everyone has a heart chakra. Holding on to fear and judgements can lead to blockages in your chakra. This is on a spiritual plane but many believe it can come up as a physical issue later. Many lessons in life are painful. Have you ever had your heart broken? Doesn't it feel like someone is crushing you inside? That pain creates trauma sometimes, and if you don't release old toxic beliefs, your chakras will hold on to that as negativity. Attachment to negative beliefs or thought patterns prevent a person's growth. That's why it's really important to forgive others. When you let go and wish the best for people even if they have hurt your spirit, you are doing yourself a huge favor. A lot of people have already been through some kind of psychological narcissistic abuse in some form. It takes time to heal. Creating affirmations and releasing feelings are therapeutic solutions. It is not a crime to take care of yourself. Practicing self-love is a vulnerable, beautiful thing and it will help you to be healthy, make wise decisions, and not participate in toxic gossip or behaviors that are low vibe. Jealousy, gossiping, or creating punishment, guilt, and shame -creates excess chaos. Let go of unrealistic expectations and reactions. Practice honesty. Listening is a good basic skill to have. Integrity, authenticity, vulnerability, compassion, mindfulness, and being easy on yourself are so important. Become aware of how you act and accept yourself for all your failures and successes - try to give yourself grace everyday. Don't hold on to the past or use it to remind others of mistakes. Instead move forward and have a positive outlook. Today is a new day!

Nice as Spice

Next up, list the things you like about yourself and the things you need to work on. My example is below so you have a rough idea.

What i like about me…..vs..what i need to work on

I am determined and motivated to accomplish my dreams.	I procrastinate at times that are important.
I have accomplished a lot by setting goals and getting them done.	Sometimes what I have accomplished seems to be enough when I know I want more.

I am persistent when I want something or when I put my mind to it.	My attention span fails me and it's hard to remember and focus.
I am social and friendly to random people.	My tendencies are to put full faith and trust into everyone until they screw me over.
I'm respectful, kind, and loyal in relationships.	I become fixated in love and attached to one person.
I am an independent self-starter.	Confidence levels are low and sometimes have self-esteem issues.
It's hard for me to give up on life and I have been told I give good vibes.	I take things personally and feel emotionally attacked when I feel like the intentions are off.
Generally I love who I am and encourage positive self-talk.	My ego and grandiosity takes over and distracts me from everything.
I make an effort to stay sober regularly	Engaging in toxic conversations
I am an animal lover and love the planet/environment	I sometimes eat unhealthy foods and don't exercise like I should
I am open-minded and strong.	When I lose trust in one person, my faith in humanity shrinks
I am a music-lover and have worldly views	It's hard for me to save money

What I like about me vs. what I need to work on

Practicing Empathy

Being Empathic comes with a lot of gratitude, compassion, and understanding how other people feel. If you identify with being an empath it means that you care about other people, try to improve the relationships, practice patience, and listen to what others have to say. Being empathetic is a side effect from loving people so much. But taking people's bullshit or letting them walk all over you is not a quality you want to have. If you don't stand up for yourself people will take advantage of you if they have malicious intent. That is where boundaries come in. It is important to be really comfortable, and therefore if something someone says or does makes you very or even a little bit uncomfortable, then you should definitely always say something. *Protect your soul/ spirit.* Sometimes it's easier to defend other people when someone is treating them unkind, than when they cross the line with *you.* You choose everyday what to share with people, including people you live with, family members, friends, or lovers. If they ask you questions, it's your choice to answer them with lies or truth, or not even answer at all. You don't have to tell people all the horny details of your life. And if someone wants to tell you something, believe me they will explain it when they feel like that is necessary, usually because they feel comfortable with you. You can tell them you are not comfortable talking about something if you need to. It seems so simple but many of us struggle. Everybody has their own set of problems to go through as well as a different walk of life. Practice empathy towards animals and communicate with them. They are so much smarter than we think. They sense and pick up on energy, we *can* communicate with them all the time. Practice sensing how your animal feels. Sit with them on the floor and make them comfortable and be with them. Pay attention to how they react with you.

A tip for handling aggression is breathing. Stop and let your body naturally let things go before you react, then you prevent "as much" explosion from something simple that went "wrong". *If you suppress your feelings, they will bottle up. If you are constantly blaming someone else, that is abusive behavior and making them your victim. Free yourself from blame, shame, and guilt. We need to learn how to stop blaming ourselves or others and finding "the fault" when something happens. Life is not happening to us, life is happening for us. Live in the moment and enjoy.*

If you have caused trauma on someone else, and it's typical we all have at some point, work on your behavior. Accept and forgive that it happened, and move on. Forgive yourself, send the person you hurt a living amends or pray for good energy and just hope the best for them. Truly hope that they are able to continue life in the most positive way. You'll feel so much better letting it go and accepting it happened. Make active steps to practice kindness on a daily basis.

Questions!!!

Do you think negative minded people can change for the better ?

If they want to . I don't think anybody has the power to change someone else. The change comes from within. There's neuroscience proving you can change the way you think. People get bad habits and childhood traumas; a lot of people blame other people or try to control them. If we all did the work on an individual level the world would be a better place. The magick starts to happen when you take the road you haven't been down before People always say What if it gets worse ? Well I say What if it gets better? - Nicole Ozburn

THE BEAUTIFUL EGO

There is really nothing wrong with being confident, feeling attractive, or good about yourself. Having a beautiful ego means you're comfortable in your own skin, not afraid to be you. So I mentioned a little bit about the fact that we can take narcissistic traits from the people around us including our family, friends, lovers, or even strangers. The good news is we can train ourselves to be different and considerate of other people's thoughts or opinions. *Healthy selfishness is okay.* We embrace our beautiful ego and respond to the vibes we receive from our Higher Selves. Listen to that inner voice. Working on yourself and loving how you are and who you are: that is finding the true empathic self. Be loving and kind to yourself and others. It is also important to protect your energy from people that have poisonous venom and do not have good intentions towards you. Maybe you feel obligated to act a certain way because they are close. But hey, if someone is making you feel like shit about yourself, what's the point of being around them? Of course it hurts to walk away but that is the best thing you can do for your starseed nature. The most powerful connection you can have with your divine higher self existence is going to be the change of your environment, and your daily routine. If you wake up and meditate, do some yoga, write something positive about yourself, or even say a prayer that you invented, you might feel that much better about your day. Accept yourself. Ask yourself, can I change and grow into something better? Let go of expectations. Sometimes we don't give ourselves enough credit for what we accomplish. Think about all the things you have done so far. It doesn't really matter if other people don't see that you are on your way to success, because you are doing it for *you*, not them. They have their own lives to worry about, so they should really mind their business unless they have some kind of positive vibes to share with you.

Keeping Up the Work

Truly love yourself, it will help you on your spiritual journey. Saying that you love yourself out loud is a great start. You can always connect through writing to your higher self. A psychic once shared with me that the "what if this happens" type thoughts stem from fear and the "I should do this."; type thoughts are from your higher self. Your higher self is your soul/spirit that is already ascended but connects to our human form in order to help us out. Each of our souls are energetically very big and have many purposes even besides your physical health. Face your fears and start over again.

You are so worth everything. You are beautiful inside and out. Anybody that doesn't agree can go ahead and step outside of this circle.

Your light is as bright as any star in the galaxies of this universe. <u>You can only shine brighter from this moment on.</u>

More positive changes are happening for the planet that will help future generations. Earth will become a world of peace and harmony one day. The laws will become less restrictive and more purposeful. Change will happen over time and everyone will find the help they need. It will be easier to live a simple lifestyle.

<u>Exercise</u> ! Get some pen and paper. *Write out something kind you can do for yourself today.* Let that be a reminder to try to do one thing for yourself each day. Examples are take a salt bath, exercise, read a chapter out of that book you haven't picked up in a while, dance for 5 minutes, walk the dog, listen to some relaxing music and meditate, call an old friend, or make a cup of tea.

Maybe we can all agree on one thing; each soul is unique. That would mean that each person on this planet earth has a different story to tell, a different reason to live for. When we have a spiritual awakening, we are lifted. We leave our old self (sinara!) behind and let go of the past traumas. We work through healing and meditation to find enlightenment. It's reassuring to find others among us with the same intentions and likeminded beauty. People that are pure and practice kindness, with no greed or ammunition ready to launch. We are one. Finding a peaceful society is closer than you think.

Your Higher Self/conscious thoughts seem to always be projecting-but sometimes we feel alone in this world. On the contrary to going through life with "Why Me?" type of thoughts, we seem to have the power as humans to change that attitude with positivity. *I accept this reality, I can handle anything.*

Love yourself enough to keep on living. It takes strength to keep moving forward. Being nice to ourselves is really the best thing we can do for us.You are a person on earth, living through karmic evolution, that deserves love. YOU are literally everything that is.

Your "Higher Self" within you is guiding you on this journey. That inner voice that tells you the right thing to do is *your* spirit. Keep your intentions in a good place. Create more affirmations like it's a hobby and make sure gratitude is still part of your routine. Believe anything can happen for you. Wait patiently, but keep making actions toward completing your goals.

Change My Life Exercise:

Here's another self love exercise. Write down what you currently would change about your life. Write down your current situation whether it is good or bad. Whether you are rich, poor, out of shape, going through a life crisis, or just wanting to improve your life. Think about anything that you can change that is in your power. Then write what you want your life to look like.

Write down in a positive affirmation the changes you have made in your life and how good it feels to have these results.

_____

_____

_____

_____

_____

_____

Now list what you have already accomplished that you can be proud of yourself for.

_____

_____

_____

_____

_____

_____

This exercise might make you put behind the negative things that have ever held you back and focus on what you can do now to help your situation.

WRITING IS SUPER HEALING AND THERAPEUTIC!!

There really is a light at the end of the tunnel, and today is your chance. Your voice is special, don't let anyone take that away from you. Your voice is important!! The truth is everyone is equal, and speaking up for yourself could save your life. Your opinion matters, share what you have to say in the best way you can. It's like when Lindsay Lohan takes the tiara at her high school prom in Mean Girls the movie, and she breaks it apart and starts tossing it out to everyone. What is the point of one person being the most beautiful, when everyone is equal?

All people come from different walks of life, and it's about what you *have* in life. It's about what you do to enjoy, and who you get to enjoy it with. *Work with what ya got.*

Toxic People in your life..

In this exercise you are going to list anyone that is toxic to your spiritual growth. This can be anyone that you feel has mistreated you in the past or maybe people affected in a situation unresolved. This could also be someone you currently have in your life or spoke to recently. Once you've made the list, think about anyone you want removed from your vibe tribe. You can still add someone if you have to see them everyday or if you must keep in your circle. The point of this exercise is to move forward with a new outlook. You'll go through each name, and answer these questions. This is just meant for you to project all your feelings towards them on paper.

Why do you feel upset when you are around this person? Why do you think your vibes don't match? Do you think their behavior sucks or they act immature? Do you feel like they act superior towards you? Is there a negative history between you two? Do you purposely hurt each other with or without intention? What bothers you the most about being around this person? Are there any boundaries you can put in place to be more comfortable around them? What can you do to channel that toxic energy into something that will free you from these thoughts?

You can answer out loud in a quiet space or write it on paper and dispose of it later.

Now you'll make a positive prayer to say outloud for that person, which will change the energy of everything. You can play some calming music in a quiet place, light a candle if you would like or some incense to set the mood.

Example 1:

_____,

I really wish things were different between us. Since I find it really hard to communicate with you, I just want to ask the UNIVERSE for closure in this relationship. I hope that your karmic lessons in life change you as a person for the good. I hope the Universe gives me karmic lessons also so that I can learn and grow. As we go our separate ways,

I release your old energy away, and sincerely let go of any ties. With love and light, our lives are separate and that old energy we shared is now gone. The universe blesses your road and I am free from any troubles of the past that involved you. Thank you Universe for showing me this new found way of thinking. Blessings and Namaste.

Example 2:

__(Henry)_____, I release your energy from my being/space because it no longer is serving me or my energetic field. I hope your journey in this karmic life is purposeful away from my presence. Thank you divine Universe for blessing this person's life and namaste, I see the light in you.

Example 1 for people that are in your circle:

My Universe collides and intercepts with your universe____ (Sue)_____, and together it would be nice if you could see that I respect you- so please do the same and we can live in peace amongst each other.

Example 2

(Patty),

I really want you to stay in my vibe tribe. I hope you find your spiritual journey to be filled with peace.Our friendship must be watered like vegetables in a garden.

Try to see your part in everything also because we are all still human. You really can't change what everyone does with their life, but you can hold yourself accountable for what you are doing in your life, and how you are treating others. Repeat the affirmations as many times as you need to, and remember your wins are valid. If you think of something that will help you, make it part of your self care routine. Try that new breathing exercise Don't be afraid to keep trying new things so you can continue to be a positive influence for yourself and others. Be creative and love yourself always.

CREATING THE CHANGE THAT NEEDS TO BE MADE….

Some days everything might go wrong and you think "The universe must have cursed me- my sock is missing!" It can be simple things that make us feel like- this kind of thing happens to ME all the time, emphasize on the *ME*. Our ego is talking and we just repeat the cycle. It's a common thing to do. We exaggerate and get overwhelmed by 1st world problems. *The more we find acceptance with our current situation and start looking at the possibilities of change, the more likely we are to take action instead of standing on the sidelines in fear.*

"The Eyes are Windows to the Soul"- *William Shakespeare*

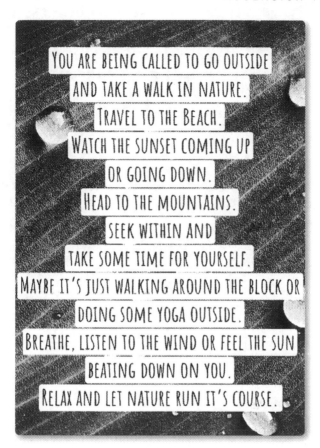

YOU ARE BEING CALLED TO GO OUTSIDE
AND TAKE A WALK IN NATURE.
TRAVEL TO THE BEACH.
WATCH THE SUNSET COMING UP
OR GOING DOWN.
HEAD TO THE MOUNTAINS.
SEEK WITHIN AND
TAKE SOME TIME FOR YOURSELF.
MAYBE IT'S JUST WALKING AROUND THE BLOCK OR
DOING SOME YOGA OUTSIDE.
BREATHE, LISTEN TO THE WIND OR FEEL THE SUN
BEATING DOWN ON YOU.
RELAX AND LET NATURE RUN IT'S COURSE.

Questions ****

<u>*What makes a person beautiful on the inside?*</u>

What I believe makes a person beautiful on the inside is how they treat others. I believe how we treat others says a lot about who we are as a person. Beauty from within has this kind, loving, and contagious aura of energy that radiates out of someone effortlessly. - *Jasmine Jackson*

CHAPTER 999

SOUL RECIPES, VITAMINS, MASSAGE, TEA, DIY CLEANING

Numbers 999: your soul is waiting for you to awaken and find yourself, do the inner work.

DRINK YOUR WATER BABE!

There was an experiment on GAIA TV in the show Superhuman: S1 Ep2 A Physical Body with Non-Physical Abilities. In this episode a woman started changing the ph levels of water by focusing her intention into it. They did the study with a DNA sample as well and the structure changed. This proves that we as humans can heal our bodies if we put our mind to it, quite literally.

Alkaline water: rich in minerals, improve bone health,neutralize acid in body

Spring water: high content of minerals like magnesium, potassium, iron, calcium, rich in oxygen, best water for you, naturally alkaline

Distilled water: no minerals in the water

Sparkling Water: heart healthy and good for digestion

Atrazine, just one common pesticide found in 95% of the USA drinking water, has been known to cause birth defects and leukemia.

To Find a Local Water Spring, visit https://findaspring.com to check out the map

Reuse your glass jars because you can store just about anything. Do not drink plastic water bottles because toxins are released into the water when the sun hits them after a period of time.

Some water brands you can trust

The Mountain Valley Spring Water sourced from The Ouachita, USA since 1871
Icelandic Glacial
Essentia
Waiakea Hawaiian Volcanic Water
VOSS
Evian

Alive Water is a natural spring water delivery service in L.A. https://alivewaters.com

Foods that are good for your soul

Avocados-omega 3 superfood, healthy mono-saturated fat, high in fiber

Brown rice-reverses High Blood Pressure and kidney ailments, also burns fat

Cashews- blood sugar level control, heart healthy

Coffee- speeds up metabolism, for anxiety and insomnia

Chard-WtF is this? - dark leafy greens good for fiber and vitamin A

Chickpeas- high in fiber, protein and healthy fats

Chili peppers- Rich in Vitamin A and C, calcium, iron, magnesium, high in Fiber

Cranberries- prevents high cholesterol, high in antioxidants, prevents UTI

Dark Chocolate-natural caffeine and causes wild dreams if eaten before bed, rich in antioxidants

Flax-good source of fiber, omega 3 fat, and produces high amount of alpha linoleic acid, inflammatory protein

Figs- contains polyphenols, antioxidant, source of fiber, oxidizes the arteries

Fish- omega 3 and 6, prevents arthritis and blood clots, lowers bad cholesterol and Triglyceride levels

Hot mustard- speeds up metabolism

<u>Kale</u>-vitamin A and reduces risk of cancer

<u>Nutritional yeast-</u> B minerals, lowers cholesterol, raises glucose tolerance, (it's so good on chickpeas)

<u>Olives</u> -high in vitamin E and powerful antioxidants

<u>Strawberries</u>-good source of fiber and keeps your teeth white

<u>Spinach</u>- burns fat, rich in iron, beta carotene, vitamin C and E, also lowers cholesterol

<u>Summer Squash</u>- helps fight cancer with antiinflammatory properties

<u>Winter Squash</u>-Vitamin c, Vitamin A, powerful antioxidant, potassium, Fiber

For the sake of your life, always eat organic or all natural !!!!!!!

If the Fruits and veggies are organic they will have a number 9 as the first number on any sticker label. Certain countries haven't created a pesticide problem so you don't always have to worry about eating organic if you're not in America. There is research in animal studies proving that pesticides are carcinogenic and cause tumors. Cancer is no joke, take your health seriously before it's too late. It is important to only consume or put on your skin products that are pesticide, petroleum, EDTA, and FREE of toxic chemicals.

Think about how vital it is to check out the nutrition facts on what you're eating or drinking. *Read the ingredients to see if it is edible.*

Choose grass fed, cage free, and LOCAL to support the community. Choose wheat bread or multigrain.

steel cut oats are a good breakfast

Saturated fat, (found in meat, egg yolk, coconut oil, palm oil, etc.) should have less than 10% of your total calories throughout the day

Stop by the Halcyon Farms stand in Oceano, CA to pick organic strawberries in the summer. They also have fresh veggies.

https://halcyonfarmsag.com

Watson's natural grocery market in Visalia, CA (Grandpa's Favorite)

They have healthy organic foods, a restaurant and a nice little patio. I love the SportsTea they have and the healthy coffee.

Growing Grounds is a nursery in San Luis Obispo that gives opportunities for careers to people with mental illness.

Order fresh produce online
from the Misfits Market, Imperfect Foods, Thrive Market,or Farm Fresh to You.

It's VITALLY important to focus on your health. And positive vibrations can go a long way, let's clean up our health and clean up the planet together.

The universe has abundant plants for everyone! We got this.

<u>SNACKS</u> people need to stay <u>WOKE</u>.

The Good Bean- Chili Lime Chickpeas
Simple Mills Farmhouse -Cheddar Almond Flour Crackers
Chameleon Organic Ground Coffee- Churro Coffee
Full Circle Organic Orange Juice
True Gold Honey- Coastal Sage Honey
Reeds Extra Ginger Beer
Fairlife Reduced Fat Milk
Zapp's Voodoo New Orleans Kettle Potato Chips- Voodoo Chips or Evil Eye Chips
Proper Wild Blackberry Clean Energy Shot
Dang Thai Rice Chips Sriracha Spice (vegan and non gmo)
Honey Mamas Oregon Mint Chocolate
Tillamook Pepper Jack Cheese
Annie Chun's-Maifun Brown Rice Noodles
Bear Naked - Triple Berry Granola
Pacific Foods- Organic Chicken Broth
Nunn-electrolyte tablets
Garden of Eatin- blue chips
Ezekiel bread

We like ethical companies <3

Suja Organic- -Suja has delicious cold-pressed juices which they make with high pressure processing to avoid bacteria, and they also have a partnership with Kiss the Ground non profit- who helps with teachings about soil for soils plus soil testing in California. -Green Delight- Suja Fuel

Taza Chocolate Company:uses certified organic cacao and are fair trade, meeting face to face with the cacao farmers. They even have a chocolate factory in Somerville, MA; and they have chocolate recipes like Mexican Hot Chocolate and Oaxaca Mole Chicken.

MIA dark chocolate : from Madagascar, the world's most indulgent vegan craft chocolate, is made in Africa, where most cocoa beans are actually grown. Their community projects include planting trees which offsets CO_2 emissions and rebuilding wildlife habitats. *ENDANGERED SPECIES CHOCOLATE*: has responsibly sourced ingredients, have made a global impact for 3 decades.10% of their net profits go towards dozens of conservation organizations.

Guayaki Yerba Mate : This company that started in San Luis Obispo is sustainable and environmentally friendly. Yerba Mate energy drinks like Orange Exuberance or Enlighten Mint have natural caffeine and organic fruit juice.The Yerba Mate plant grows in the South American rainforest, and is harvested by small farms and indigenous communities in Paraguay, Argentina, and Brazil. It is a healthy tea with 24 vitamins and minerals.

Clean Cause. Yerba Mate energy drinks: 50% of profits SUPPORT ADDICTION RECOVERY. These are low sugar, contain vitamins, prebiotics, and provide a long lasting buzz (wink wink)

With all that snacking, comes lots of packaging.

It's 2023 and there are now solutions to everything up the wing-wong!! Meaning: start avoiding contributing to those landfills and start converting to a zero- waste system in your house!

Composting your veggies and eggshells into your garden is a start. The next best option is to get those hands on a Lasso Loop. This is a badass recycling machine that everyone should own. It scans and recycles all different materials and disintegrates them down to dust, and you only have to change it out 3-8 times a year. *Lomi* is a composting machine for food waste that creates healthy rich soil for your garden.

Basil-Repels white flies and mosquitos, basil and thyme among cucumbers and squash keeps away worms.

Rosemary and sage also keeps away moths . Geranium and Eucalyptus oil keep the bugs away.

Soul Recipes

Breakfast

Monk Coffee 2 Go
Whole Foods 365 instant espresso
Organic Half and Half
Monk Fruit in the Raw 1 packet

Have a great day!

California Avo Toast
Rustik Oven sourdough bread
Pesto
½ avocado
2 scrambled eggs
shredded mexican blend cheese
Wicked Winona the perfect blend seasoning

Make toast, make 2 eggs, spread pesto, avocado, slap the eggs on sprinkle cheese and seasoning

Happy Morning Gorgeous

Feta & Eggs
Kale
Feta Cheese crumbled
Eggs
Pesto
Naan Bread

Make eggs, add kale, add feta and melt for a second, spread the pesto on that naan and slap the rest on then call it a day!

Grandpa's Overnight Oatmeal <3
Oatmeal
Flax
Spoonful of turmeric
Chia seeds
Coconut Milk
Blueberries

Leave everything except blueberries together overnight, add them berries in the A.M

Now that's a good breakfast ;)

Juicing

Morning Feel Good Shot
1 clove of garlic
Ginger
½ of a Lemon
Turmeric
20 drops Colloidal Silver

Great immunity booster!

Anti-Sick Shot
Fresh Ginger
½ lime
½ cucumber
1 clove garlic
½ grapefruit
20 drops colloidal silver

Smoothies

Strawberry Smoothie
Fairlife whole milk
Organic strawberries
Banana

Kale
Ice
½ frozen strawberry fruit popsicle

Party Treats

Date Me! Goat Cheese Bacon Dates
Coconut covered dates
Goat cheese
Bacon

Cut a tray of dates open and stuff with goat cheese, wrap in bacon and cook in the oven for 10 minutes

Enjoy

Favorites

Mermaid Seaweed Pesto Pasta
Blue Evolution Seaweed Penne wheat pasta with sea lettuce (plant based iodine and earth friendly)
Pesto
Olive oil
Parmesan
Full Circle raw Spinach
Organic yellow squash

Boil water, cook pasta, strain with cold water

Add olive oil and chop up squash then throw it in~add pesto, spinach ~once squash is cooked add parmesan and enjoy!

Kick Ass Bruschetta
The Rustik Oven Sourdough Bread
Tillamook White Cheddar
Tillamook Chives and Onion Cream Cheese
California Sun- sun dried tomato bruschetta
Gallo Salame Italian Dry
TSAGLIS (greek) Dry Extra Virgin Olive Oil
McCormick Gourmet Organic Herbes De Provence

Bake and Enjoy <3

Kat's Yummy Lentil Soup
Half a bag of lentils
Free range chicken broth
Rosemary
Herbs de vore
Chili powder
1 can marinated artichokes
5 pieces cooked bacon
Grilled onions
Mediterranean herbs
A dash of black pepper and salt

Boil Water, add lentils and chicken broth
In a separate pan cook bacon, add all the rest in and enjoy!

Salads

Bake-Me Croutons
Oasis whole wheat bread
Ghee oil
Seaweed salt blend
Braggs 24 herb blend

Cover pan with ghee oil
Cut Bread into squares
Season and Bake on 350 for 10 mins, toss them around halfway through

Eat-Me Apple Celery Salad (pretend you're at Olive Garden lol)
1 gala apple
Organic celery chopped
2 petite cucumbers
Spinach
Abby's Kitchen Italian Dressing
1 can mandarins
1 can garbanzo beans
Cabot alpine cheddar cheese, shredded
Go Raw salad topper
Bake-Me Croutons

Chop, Mix, add croutons and toppings !

Live it up

Veganism and vegetarian diets are great for increasing chances of being cancer-free. If you go this route you will definitely want to take Vitamin D, Vitamin B-12, and pay attention to your protein levels. It's good to incorporate more veggies and fruits into your diet while getting your protein. Choose what feels good.

Vitamins and Minerals

Something else that compliments your nutrition is vitamins. Whether you think they work or have never tried them, there is scientific research to prove that many supplements are beneficial. Being a massage therapist, I have heard many stories of people trying holistic remedies and having great *success.*

Brain Health

Fish oil- omega 3s, brain development
Ginseng- memory improvement
Ginkgo Biloba- antioxidants, memory function
Lion's Mane Mushroom- reduce inflammation in brain, cognition
NAC- regulate glutamate levels which involves behavior and memory function

Anxiety and Sleep Aids

Ashwagandha- relieves stress, supports heart health
Valerian Root-treats insomnia and depression
Lemon Balm-calms nerves and anxiety, improves appetite
Chamomile- sleep aid, digestive relaxant
Kava Kava- for anxiety/stress, elevates mood

Passionflower-anxiety/sleep, improves heart rhythms
Lavender-calming, sleeping aid, prevents anxiety

Upset Stomach

Peppermint oil to breathe in and peppermint tea- relieves nausea and headaches, also prevents lactation
Ginger- nausea, motion sickness, increases dopamine and serotonin
Aloe Vera Juice- aids digestion, constipation, heals wounds
Probiotics- fights bad bacteria so you can have a healthy gut
Prebiotics- food for probiotics so they can thrive (you want to create that good bacteria to fight virus and toxins)

Immunity

Vitamin C- growth and repair of all body tissues
Zinc- immunity, blood clotting, essential for taste and smell
Elderberry Syrup- immune support, colds, cough
Echinacea- throat comfort, prevents asthma, pain killer
Oil of Oregano- great for immunity, antibiotic
Black garlic- fights free radicals, healthy immune system

Menstruation/Sex health

Raspberry Leaf Tea- supports late stage of pregnancy, morning sickness
Dong quai- relieves cramps, regulates irregular menstrual cycles
Mugwort- menstrual cramps, child-birth, and menopause

<u>Chasteberry</u>- hormone function
<u>Evening primrose oil</u> - increases cervical mucus
<u>Cinnamon</u>- sperm production
<u>Ashwagangha-</u> increases sperm count
<u>Saw Palmetto</u>-supports men's sex hormones
<u>Longjack (Tongkat Ali)</u>- boosts testosterone levels, aphrodisiac

For hormonal health, watch your diet by adding protein and less carbs. Do metabolic workouts. Add in foods that produce progesterone like kale, pumpkin, grapefruit and brussel sprouts. Add saffron oil supplement or tea for a mood booster.

Fun Fact: Neem Oil kills sperm when applied topically before intercourse and has been known as a natural contraceptive in India. Tracking your ovulation each month can give you a better idea of when you are most fertile, for anyone trying to get pregnant or not trying.

<u>For thyroid problems-take iodine for hypothyroidism-or also take an iron supplement.</u>

Skin

<u>Aloe vera </u>helps heal a wound or burn, of course treat sunburns
<u>Tea tree</u> antifungal, treats dandruff, antiseptic
<u>Neem oil</u> antifungal and helps with itchiness
<u>Coconut Oil-</u> antifungal
<u>Colloidal Oatmeal</u>- eczema

Calendula- soft skin

First Aid

Colloidal Silver: when applied topically can help treat HPV-2, used to treat ear infections, pink eye, wounds
Tecnu Poison Oak- removes poison oak oils
Iodine- cleaning wounds

Pain Management

Tiger balm- manage pain, tension headaches
Menthol- chronic pain
Arnica- for arthritic pain, inflammation
Turmeric- inflammation
Willow bark- headaches, pain, inflammation
Mugwort- Soldiers used to put mugwort in the bottom of their shoes to relieve aching. It can be used as a poultice, which is the herb in a damp cloth placed wherever there is inflammation

An Epsom Salt Bath can really help relax your muscles, release toxins, and as a major plus raise your vibration to clear your energy just when those vampires are planning their next attack (hehe) (empath humor)

Kats High Vibe Muscle Soak Salts:

Epsom salt
Himalayan salt
Eucalyptus oil
A scoop of lavender

Mix, put in a mason jar, and chill the frack out!

Ice Baths and **Cold Showers** increase dopamine levels.

Healing

Ask Archangel Raphael for green healing energy and praying for healing. Practice Reiki and do positive affirmations to get in the mindset you need. "I am healing. My body is perfect as it is. I love my body." Thank your body for being amazing and tell yourself in the mirror that you love yourself. When you speak about your body to other people, always be positive about it and practice good self-talk.

HEAL
YOUR MIND FIRST.
MIND BODY SPIRIT

Massage

Your muscles are made up of fascia, which is the layers of muscle tissue in the body. Regular massage can help to break up this tissue when tension and stress has made your muscles tighten up. It's important to drink plenty of water after a massage to flush out all the toxins that are released. The benefits of Swedish massage are increased circulation and blood flow to the muscles, enhance mood, increase energy, reduce stress. The benefits of deep tissue massage include reducing chronic pain, breaking up scar tissue, reduces inflammation, lowers blood pressure and heart rate, and creates mobility in the body.

Other tips for when you feel a cold coming on or you just want to get ahead of the game with an immunity boost:

Eat a clove of garlic/black garlic
Clear sinuses: hot peppers, wasabi, sinus inhalers, neti pot, eucalyptus
Put a few drops of Thieves oil by Young Living or On Guard by Doterra into your water (also great for cleaning/diffuser) for immunity
Extra Vitamin C, Zinc, and Vitamin D
The Wellness Formula (wink wink works every time)
Hot tea with lemon
Chicken Bone Broth or hot soups with veggies like Pho
Colloidal Silver boosts immunity put tincture in water and drink
L-Lysine - block infections, improve immune function

Random Tip: to open up the sinuses, bring water to boil then add 10 drops of Peppermint and Eucalyptus each. Place a towel over your head to trap in the steam as you take full breaths inhaling deeply. I did this one night when I couldn't sleep and couldn't breathe through my nose; it's literally magick!

Great Supplement Brands (you can trust!)

Bragg's- Apple Cider Vinegar

Source Natural- The Wellness Formula *(some people take this daily, it's amazing and always gets rid of a nasty cold!)*

BlissRiver Organics- Elderberry Syrup *(bonus: tastes like candy!)*

Planetary Herbals- Old Indian Wild Cherry Bark Syrup *(works miracles) (instead of NyQuil)*

Garden of Life- Women's or Men's Daily vitamins with probiotics *(fun fact: the founder originally sold carrot juice and kefir everyday to start his business)*

GT's Synergy - Sacred Life Trilogy Kombucha *(in case the sober folks are interested 8 bottles of kombucha is equal to one beer) (p.s it's extremely dangerous to drink that much kombucha in one sitting lol) (p.s not recommended)*

OLLY- Laser Focus, with Ginseng (for thinking fast)

They don't use artificial ingredients, just natural flavors which make the gummy taste like a tiny snack

It's really important to support ethical companies instead of mainstream corporate business that create slavery and human trafficking in other countries and include toxic harmful chemicals in products that some people consider to be edible.

*QUESTION TIME *

What is self love or self care to you?

I get a massage once a week and if I can't afford it, then I'll go two times a month or use my handheld massager. You have to have blood flow. I think massage is big and it helped me get through things in life and was my stress reliever. I get a pedicure and that also makes me feel pampered.

-Sandy Sandoval

What do you do, to express your love for yourself? It might be saying I love you in the mirror, working out, or making a cup of tea. What do you do for yourself that makes you appreciate just being you?

_____

_____

Try this exercise. Write down your answer. By
What is one thing that I can eliminate from my diet this week, that is toxic to my body anyway?

_____

What is one exercise I can add to my daily routine this week to strengthen my body?

_____

What is one thing I can add to a recipe or snack this week that will help nourish my body?

_____

Remember to drink water babe!

Tea Time!

"We're all Mad here. I'm mad. You're mad."- says the Cat from Alice and Wonderland by Jane Carruth

Green Tea: prevents growth of cancerous cells, burns fat, prevents clogging of arteries, reduces stress and risks of strokes, improves cholesterol levels

Black Tea: highest caffeine content, protects lungs

White Tea: most potent anti cancer properties

Oolong: weight loss

Pu-erh Tea: reduces cholesterol

Chamomile Tea: prevents complications from diabetes, stunts growth of cancer cells

Many say tea was discovered by Buddha himself

Pear Tea Lemonade

½ bottle pink lemonade
Pear juice
3 bags *Yogi* Passionfruit Green Tea
1 can grapefruit sparkling water
Spring water
½ lime

Mix everything in pitcher and let tea bags sit for a few hours in fridge

Summertime Chill Vibes

Kat's Homemade Yerba Mate

Guayaki Yerba mate tea loose leaf
Lemon
Lime
Monk fruit or honey

Hot or Cold <3

Lemon Peppermint Iced Tea

¼ lemon
Peppermint or spearmint leaves in a tea ball
Spring water
Honey

Makes 1 Cup, Make your day worth it :)

<u>Household</u> <u>Cleaning</u>

At least people are making a decent effort at striving towards using more humane household cleaning products, but a lot of companies that are putting a "natural" face on their product, still have preservatives that are really harmful in their ingredient list.

EWG - Environmental Working Group (<u>www.EWG.org</u>) is a great website to learn about everyday products that are harmful. Lookup any brand to see the truth about what chemicals cause cancer and skin allergies.

<u>You got DIY Options!</u>

Think about how much money you can save making your own spray blend, while avoiding putting cancerous lethal chemicals into your lungs. The FDA doesn't give a damn about your livelihood: it's all about the money. It's your choice what products you surround yourself with: quite literally.

Use a glass cleaning bottle spray (*Grove* has a great one) to create your own disinfectant, glass spray, or stove cleaner!

Essential Oils for Cleaning

Lemon- eliminates mold
Tea Tree- antiseptic
Lavender-disinfectant
Eucalyptus- antibacterial
Pine- antimicrobial

<u>Steam Mopping</u>
Warm water
Dish soap
Essential oils

<u>Fresh Air Room spray</u>
Vodka (Substitute vodka for vinegar or water)
Essential oils

<u>Household Disinfectant</u>
Lemon and Lavender oil
Vinegar
Pine needles or citrus peel

Make your own Laundry detergent using white Vinegar, Baking soda, or Hydrogen peroxide with essential oils. Many so-called natural cleaning product companies use very toxic preservatives that can cause allergic reactions and eczema. There is hardly any decent laundry detergent that doesn't have harmful ingredients to the skin (funny how that's even legal). Instead of switching to natural detergent, make your own!

<u>DIY dish soap</u>
1 part Vinegar
1 part Warm water
Essential oils
Castile soap

Tips: when making at home products: do not mix baking soda and vinegar, it will create salt which will be useless for cleaning. Do not mix bleach and vinegar because it will create toxic fumes.

Here are some eco-friendly household items you'll want to put in the shopping cart
Wool dryer balls (prevents static)
Rebel plant based window cleaner
<u>Galaxy Green</u> Bamboo Bath Tissues
(Fun fact: Bamboo Trees grow back within one year, and material made from bamboo is as soft as hell.)

<u>Seventh Generation</u> lavender disinfectant aerosol

Life Hack: half of a lemon mixed with baking soda can be applied to your car headlights as a cleaner: leave for 5 mins then remove it works like a charm! (Or use baking soda toothpaste)

Around the house..

In Indonesia, Feng Shui is a regular practice and it would be beneficial for people around the world to practice it also. This is about attracting luck or prosperity in different areas of your home and strategically moving things around, making room for new space. Clear Your Clutter with Feng Shui by Karen Kingston is a great reference. Learn where to place your bed to keep harmony and leave the space behind your doors empty to bring new opportunities in.

Marie Kondo's book *Spark Joy* will help you declutter and find organization methods that make life easier. Once you get started, it becomes a natural habit to start putting things where they belong and where you will find them.

<u>Our Can Crushing Reality</u>

The universe provides so many everlasting materials for us to harvest in nature, and humans continue to enslave each other for consumer goods, without using sustainable methods of production. But on the bright side, we are creating recyclable products even more as the people of the universes' preference nowadays. Corporations want us to believe that we <u>need</u> that fake perfume or bag of hot cheetos with commercials and propaganda. It is sad that all those types of efforts are permanently wasted, because in truth people want quality and want to live longer. The evilness and power of mass production has affected the world. Local goods used to be the only way people survived, and in a way we have lost our sense of community. It's a straight up tooth for tooth war out there. The rainforest is practically gone now. There are millions of pieces of plastic trash floating around the ocean, affecting marine life and pollution. This planet needs our help, and the time it takes for these resources to grow back isn't an instant process. If we keep making small steps, slow and steady progress, the world will know a more peaceful way of living.

Companies makings strides
The Nature Conservancy
Green Peace
DOCTORS WITHOUT BORDERS (gave out the covid vaccination in 3rd world countries during pandemic.)

CHAPTER 11:11

MAGICK, BEAUTY, HERBS, AND YOGA

Woo-hoo, witchy woman
See how high she flies
Woo-hoo, witchy woman
She got the moon in her eyes
Witchy Woman by The Eagles

Witch Please!

Witchcraft is essentially about altering energy with the power of *intention* to make your desires come true. The ingredients in my spells are just *suggestions*. Traditionally witches used what they could find for spells, which is less wasteful anyway. If you have different herbs or crystals.. don't think that you have to hunt down some Schizandra Berry to fit in. If you want to do a spell with a bag of grapes and a fruitcake candle, by all means you do you boo. If you don't have your own coven yet, you can practice magick on your own. Magick is truly about intention and working with nature. Just think of your wishes and desires and how you can start manifesting that reality. I'm a baby eclectic witch still and there is so much to learn. *The Universe listens to everything: it's like the government but better and bigger. Your guides are protecting you and listening to your requests. All they ask for is a thank you every once in a while. Abundance is naturally yours- start believing it can happen for **you.***

<u>Spirit Animals</u>

When you see a certain animal passing you by or coming up to you randomly, crossing the road, etc, ***it is a sign from the universe/your guides.*** Pay attention when it happens and look up the spiritual meaning for that animal totem. You will be surprised at how relevant it is to your life.

<u>Mosquito</u>: survival, persistence, perception

<u>Coyote</u>: survival, adaptability, tenacity, resourcefulness, and cleverness

<u>Butterfly</u>: always evolving

<u>Dragonfly</u>: quick changes in your life

<u>Wolf</u>: navigate through life with strength and confidence

The Tarot

There are SO many tarot/Oracle decks to choose from nowadays. Tarot is a form of divination, understanding your fate. The original Rider Waite gypsy deck has a history. It was a game that Romanian gypsies played that turned into reading each other's fortunes. Travelers told a story through the deck and each card became more powerful and accurate. The tarot originally has 72 cards, a major arcana and minor arcana. I will give you the basic meanings of a few of my favorite cards.

The Sun: positivity, enlightenment, Sun energy, providing for all, a person in your life or you giving a

Positive impact, gratitude, happiness

The Star: a card of gratitude, having everything you need in life

The Hermit: insight, looking within, seeking wisdom, nature

Self- Love Clearing Ritual

*play Dreams by Fleetwood Mac

You'll need:

-mugwort *(psychic dreams)*
-a bay leaf or two! *(wishes fulfilled)*

Write your birthdate on one side and positive affirmations on the other like- "you go girl", "you got this", or "love you"

Dragon's Blood Resin *(brings power to spells)*

Lavender *(protection)*

Put all ingredients in a bowl where you can burn everything (cauldron Mwhahahaha)

> Wear a necklace that is special to you. *(Clear the energy of it before you put it on)* Create a circle of salt around yourself and the bowl for protection.
> Light the bay leaf, dragon's blood, lavender and mugwort in the safe bowl.
> Oh yeah! Do this outside or open the windows.
>
> "In this sacred space, I stay true to you and walk with you around ancient herbs of healing (walking), May joy be brought to my soul and I thank the Divine!"

Thank your spirit guides
Kiss the pendant of the necklace you are
wearing
And let everything burn
Xo

(Dance to *dreams*) :)

<u>*A Love Charm for Soulmates in the Universe;*</u>

may they find peace, harmony, and romantic love.

<u>You will need:</u>

Small glass bottle or bottles
Cords or necklace chokers
Glitter
Candle wax
Salt (*protection*)

<u>Herbs:</u>

Lavender (*brings inner peace*)
Hibiscus (*love*)
Rose petals (*love*)
Marigold (*prophetic dreams*)
Cinnamon (*attracts love in a powerful way*)
Peppermint oil (*welcomes love and protection*)
Patchouli oil (*aphrodisiac*)
Eucalyptus oil (*healing*)
Cernunnos and Jupiter incense from *The Brass Unicorn, Fresno, Ca (metaphysical shop)*

Create an intention or prayer. Mine was asking the universe to bring peace and harmony to my relationships and for everyone in the universe to find their soulmates. Sage the room and yourself. Start by making a beautiful altar with love letters, images of animals in love, the person you love and you, tealights, roses,the lovers card in the tarot deck, anything symbolizing love to you. You can make a batch of charms like I did or just one.

Sage the inside of the glass bottle or use palo santo or salt at the bottom. Add oil around the rim, then mix herbs and add to the bottle, seal with candle wax then add glitter.

You can make necklaces out of them like I did, gifts for your friends, carry the charm with you to attract love, or put them on your altar at home.

Thank you Universe for granting this and for everyone in the collective consciousness to be blessed in love, harmony, and peace.

<3

SHADOW WORK

<u>Biggest Fears change into positive exercise!!!</u>

Grab a pen and paper. List all of your deepest, darkest fears. Think of everything you've ever imagined that gives you that gut punching eerie feeling, whether it's ways of dying or just the worst thing that can happen to you.

Now that you've listed each fear, you are going to change it into a positive.

Example 1:

I want to be loved/known/remembered and I scare myself by imagining I die alone and as a nobody.

Positive Change: People already love you, you'll be someone, believe me.

Example 2:

I imagine a car accident specifically driving off a cliff.

Positive change:

Drive safe!! You're fine. You'll be fine, always pay attention to the road and the energy of people driving.

See how this works?

Another way to fight your fears is to really just imagine that fear actually happening to you. Just think your fear is to be naked in front of the world. Visualize it really happens. So what? So was it really that bad? A lot of times our fears are so outlandish and *if* it really came true, it wouldn't be the end of the world. Especially if you're a cat and have 9 lives, that helps quite a bit.

Shadow-work is about self work. Instead of staying in guilt or shame, be playful with yourself and cut yourself some slack. Channel it into motivation. Meet your goals one at a time and stay connected with your higher self.

<u>Guided Meditation for attracting abundance</u>
Imagine a Bowl of money.
Or even take some money from your purse, (*If you have any.)
Now put it in a jar or bowl
And Sing with me
I am beautiful
I am Loved
I am Worth it
Because I am a F*cking masterpiece

<u>Self Love</u>
I am worth it.
I am a beautiful Bad B!tch.
Etc.

<u>Self-Care Consistency</u>
It's time to really start loving yourself. Like the stars have aligned, align your mind, body, and spirit with your Brain!!!
Align your chakras.
Align your life.
Shine with all your might, you are growing already.
Eat Healthy.
Exercise.
Get inspired by and motivated to be better. You can always do better!

Whatever you are struggling with, put health, relationships, wealth, success, and spiritual practices first.

Herbs for Magick
For your rituals, spellcrafting, healing, beauty and medicinal uses.

Mugwort(Artemisia)common wormwood: magical properties of Divinity, named after Greek Moon Goddess Artemis, perennial, used in europe as a tonic before hops, protection for women and travelers, prevents nightmares and aids in a peaceful sleep,-the parts you can use are the flowering tops and leaves.

Bay leaves- great to use to attract money-write on the back your birthdate and reasonable amount of money you want to receive and then burn in safe space/a bowl

Sage -clearing your space, cleansing all toxic negative energy into the light, can be used in essential oil form, use the sticks to clear your energy, the energy of your house which is similar to feng shui techniques

Essential Oils
Rose-aphrodisiac
Lavender: relaxation, antiseptic, calming
Patchouli: aphrodisiac

You can always burn incense in the car or outside. And natural candles made with essential oils are the best way to go, to avoid those damn Glade things. It is really awful to breathe in a bunch of chemicals when you could just buy or make a soy candle that smells way better anyway.

Incense

Palo Santo -grounding
Copal-awakening

Beauty

BATHING IN BEAUTIFUL INGREDIENTS!!

It's not as hard as you think to make your own sprays, lotions, toothpaste, shower gel, etc. Let's get back to the roots of our ancestors who used natural beauty secrets before "toxins were cool". What makes you pretty is your inner beauty, *your soul*.

Homemade beauty recipes

<u>DIY Deodorant</u>
Vodka
Lavender oil
Peppermint oil
Eucalyptus oil

<u>Kat's Body Butter</u>
Shea Butter
Coconut oil
Mandarin Vanilla Body Lotion by Andalou
Jojoba oil
Avocado oil
Grapefruit Essential Oil
Sweet Almond oil

<u>Kats massage oils</u>
(Create your own with a carrier oil and essential oils)

<u>Hippie Sauce</u>
Jojoba oil - closest oil to the oil that our skin naturally produces
A few drops of Patchouli oil

<u>Orange and Cinnamon</u>
Almond oil
A few drops of Orange oil
A few drops of Cinnamon oil - good for blood pressure

<u>Kats sugar body scrub</u>
Organic brown sugar
Honey
Lavender flower
Coconut oil

<u>Lube</u>
Aloe Vera

That's it!

<u>Face mask</u>
Greek Yogurt and honey
That's it!

<u>Toothpaste</u>
Lemon or orange zest
1 teaspoon Baking soda
Peppermint oil
Clove oil
1 teaspoon Bentonite Clay
1 tbsp coconut oil

<u>Mouthwash</u>
Gargle with warm water Himalayan salt

P.S Clove oil on cavities works amazing

Peppermint oil on toothbrush for fresh breath

Divine Masculine Spray
Water
Tiny bit of alcohol
Pine oil
Sandalwood oil
Eucalyptus oil

Love Potion #9 (divine feminine spray)
Libra full moon water (mason jar under the moon)
Cinnamon
Lavender
Rosewater

Inhaling toxic perfume is not hot on anyone: and it gives us all a headache!

P.S everyone should own a tongue scraper, a pumice stone, facial extractors, a foot file, a neti pot, facial steamer, a Yoni/Lingam steamer, nose breathing strips, nostril inhalers, incense, a fruit roll up, and good vibes. :)

Yoni steaming/Lingham

Steaming benefits include healthy blood flow, fights bacteria, increases fertility, support urinary health, prostate health, natural detoxification, restore reproductive system, and bring oxygen to the reproductive system. For yoni, great herbs are mugwort, lavender, and peppermint. For Lingham steaming, Saw Palmetto, and Yarrow.

It feels so good and helps you feel great *down there*!

More tips..

Highlight your hair with squirts of lemon juice and bathe in the sun. You can also color your hair naturally with henna or **Arctic Fox**.

Use a foot file to file down those rough edges of your feet, and a real pumice rock to smooth your heels. Foot peels are also great for removing dead skin.

And life is too short to have a bra with a wire in it!

Don't let *anyone* mess up your vibe or your style. If anyone doesn't love how you look with a big T-Shirt and some comfy slippers,*they* are the problem, not you. Cosmetics are an artistic and fun outlet where you can be creative and passionate about colors. Whatever you are into, don't stop being who you are because of someone else's opinion. Obviously the world has shifted and any gender wears makeup if they want to.

Everyone is Beautiful.

What's hot in 2023? ***Kindness.*** You can deny it all you want but most people are done with the **B***S*****! Doing good things on purpose and being nice to people? *That* is sexy and attractive. Your appearance is **extra**, something to express. Obviously though it is very healthy to take care of your hair, skin, and nails and upkeep on hygiene. It can be frustrating when formaldehyde and trashy ingredients are legally sold and advertised for people to put all over themselves without thinking twice. Before plastic surgery (which can cause cancer, permanent damage, and unnecessary guilt and shame if used for non-medical reasons) became the thing to do, **natural** was all there was.

Natural is still beautiful and there are plenty of brands out there changing ingredients, resources, and packaging in a **pro-planet** manner. The beauty world seems to be changing for the better, meaning less harsh chemicals and unnecessary ingredients. If you are using clean ingredients you don't have to worry about popular toxic formulas breaking out your skin. Even when you try really hard to get natural beauty products, you can still make the mistake of trusting brands that add chemicals causing health problems in the long run.

These legitimate brands you can trust don't contain anything evil. They are environmentally sweet and are making good choices for Earth:

Pacifica Gardenia perfume offers all natural sustainable beauty products

100% PURE Maracuja Oil mascara helps your real eyelashes grow and lengthen.

They also have eye cream with coffee bean extract for those super tired mornings.

Gabriel makeup- all natural foundation, mascara, eyeliner <3

Mineral Fusion makeup- nail polish, cover up

<u>Soap=Hope</u> gives someone in need a bar of soap for every bar of soap that you buy. They are also sustainable and ethical.

***The book Renegade Beauty* by Nadine Artemis** is absolutely women empowerment and the beauty bath bomb you need.

Yoga has literally caught on in America like freaking wildfire and everybody has tried it nowadays or at least some basic stretching. Yoga makes you feel amazing. There is Vinyasa Flow which is a hardcore workout, Restorative which is relaxing and mostly seated poses, Bikram (hot yoga), Bhakti (heart yoga that is community driven), kundalini yoga, tantric yoga (couples therapy), Yin yoga (holding poses for longer period), Hatha yoga (gentle flow) and much more. It's a great workout that engages all muscles of the body. And it's meditative. At the end of a yoga class it's important to have Savasana, which concludes your practice with rest and meditation. I would recommend Yoga with Adrienne, Kundalini yoga with Kimilla, Boho Beautiful, Beach Yoga Girl, Yoga for Men, and Movement by Mary Angeline on YouTube.

Moon Magic

Get *intentional* about having a ritual around the moon. An intention is having a freaking purpose to your magic. Why are you doing it and what do you want to achieve? The possibilities are endless! Absorb the energy of the moon for your spells and ask your higher self for guidance. Simply write down an intention on a piece of paper then put it in a jar under the full moon. The moon is continuously in a different zodiac sign. So if it's a Pisces New Moon (for example), think what would you like to do/create to harness that energy? New Moons are powerful for closure, renewals, and rebirth. Full Moons are for manifestations and releasing something quickly. Stay ahead of the game and be prepared for how you can incorporate the magic of the moon into your life by drinking Moon Water, charging your crystals under the moon or in moon water, full moon bonfire, and renewing your soul with ritual.

Check out the *Manifest Station Yoga Studio* in Fresno, CA, where they have women's moon circles with yoga, guided meditation, and snacks with open-heart conversations once a month.

Lunarly is a subscription box if you want to learn about the moon, receive crystals and candles. Lunarly gives you a card in your self care box with the upcoming specific moon phase for that month.

I LOVE SAILOR MOON, GREENMAN, AND ODIN. <3 and Jakey!!!

May all black cats (and all cats) and dogs be happy campers and magical pets.

CHAPTER 13

RANDOM <3 REFLECTION

Whether you consider yourself to be hella weird or totally fracking normal; there is a place for you on earth.

Questions!!

What makes your soul happy?

My souls happy place I must say is anywhere alongside my handsome man. He brings my spirit and soul protection, peace, and a state of calm. By him doing so it allows me to be the best version of myself I strive to be everyday. He is my number supporter and this is why I love him so much..lol. -Jasmine Jackson

My personal relationship to a *higher power*:

The divine connection to source, the highest frequency of light, which I call the spirit of the universe, creator of the light and dark. For me, it's the spirit of the universe, my angels/demons/spirit guides, and higher vibration I am connected with. I fully believe that there is a plan for me and everyone else.

Ascension is what it's like to live in the clouds.

So I made friends with all my demons
Let 'em sink their teeth in
Got used to the feeling of letting it go
So give me something to believe in
Or throw me in the deep end
It all feels the same with your eyes closed
So you can throw me in the
Deep end (deep)
Deep end (deep end)
Deep end (deep)
Deep end

Song by I Prevail
"Deep End"

For the love of being a hippie..

Ama The Hugging Saint is a guru and humanitarian (https://amma.org/) that is known for her selfless love by comforting more than 34 million people. She's like Mother Teresa reincarnated (and on my list of people I want to meet). She has been asked where she gets the energy to help so many people, and Ama has replied, "Where there is true love, anything is effortless." If one person can spiritually change that many lives, what can a whole community of like minded individuals accomplish?

If the Dali Lama was running this country, we might have an actual sufficient way of recycling, successful home grown businesses and communities, where nonviolence is actually something to strive for.

Vote for Kennedy!

Gamers

Video games have a positive future that is not only magical but uplifting and stimulating. Ariana Grande in Fortnite is super cool and spiritual. There is a company called TRU LUV that is changing the "gaming" industry into an environment of positivity, grounding nature, meditative and calming thoughts, love for yourself, and less stress and more productive thinking. The app they created is called #SelfCare. #SelfCare is cute because you basically can do fun brain activities, pet your virtual black cat that sleeps in your virtual bed, right next to your virtual plants, and even play with your virtual tarot cards that hold different meanings to your heart. *Fantasy is everything.*

Crystal Clear

Clear the energy of your things and your phone/devices by saging your phone and asking your guides to protect your vibration. You can ask them to clear your phone or put a circle of salt around it for a few hours.

Affirmation

"My phone is cleansed with positive vibes and I attract the good energy that uplifts me."

Create your own prayer or a protection affirmation. I looked up the prayer for La Santa Muerte and said it aloud to honor her, and in a way now I have her protection guiding me and any activities from my phone if that makes sense.. Since we are cleansing our phones, a good way to close would be to call on your favorite saint of protection so that when you are engaging with your phone, the energy is on the same level as what you are trying to attract from the universe. Instead of using an altar, these phones are actually pretty cool because you can look up a prayer or a picture of a deity and honor them by setting your phone down and lighting a candle with them for a few minutes.

I ASK THE UNIVERSE to bless my phone and attract positive light, loving vibrations. People want to contact me with good intentions and I deserve respect. This circle of salt/sage/crystal/(or just good vibes) represents my divine intuitive nature and my device is now energetically clean. I ask for all of the functions of this phone to be as sweet as honey. Thank you divine universe for cleansing this energy that is a magnet for luck, love, success, high frequency news, and pleasure."

ASMR stands for "Autonomous Sensory Meridian Response". It creates a tingly feeling throughout the body, by listening to different sounds on a microphone such as tapping, soft voice, or various methods to relax for the person watching. It really helps people with anxiety and ASMR TikTok Lives will relieve sleepless nights due to fear and stress.Reading,infrared heated yoga, my sound machine with ocean waves, bath fizzies, face masks,eye pillows, and essential oils are also super helpful for me personally.

Universal Clothing Exchange

Shopping or donating at thrift stores often can help charities, people in need, and score on great items that are sometimes brand new. According to the International Labor Organization, an estimated 170 million children are engaged in child labor from picking cotton to spinning yarn to creating clothing. The countries this clothing industry is coming from are Bangladesh, India, Pakistan, Egypt, China, Thailand, and Uzbekistan. The reality is people in these countries are working for hardly nothing, then their kids have to start picking cotton or making clothes which prevents them from having an education, stuck in a poverty whirlpool.

Calling all that "convenience" is terrifying and contributing. There are solutions that exist already.

The *Global Organic Textile Standard* lists different clothing shops from around the world you can support that are ethical using sustainable materials. In San Luis Obispo, California, there are two companies I know of; *Humankind Fair Trade* and *Eco Bambino* for infants. *Global Fashion Exchange* is a company that creates worldwide clothing exchange events and brand transformation. *Smartwool* recycles used socks and makes them into brand new hiking socks and other clothing! Checkout *Grateful Threads* in Grover Beach for the best consignment store ever, you won't regret it!

What's happening in the world?

Some countries are not using technology at the same pace as others because they are not developing at the same speed economically and so on. Apps like *Quartz* and *Al Jazeera* give information on global news based on research and facts rather than opinion. Try not to get caught up in social media madness, celebrity stories, and political stuff. Having your own opinion doesn't mean everyone thinks the same way as you. If we can help it, we should be more genuine and respectful to each other. Let's face it. We are not some utopian society where people don't ever think of punching someone else right where it hurts. We can imagine pretty rainbows and dragons all we want, but unfortunately there is a crisis of human and animal starvation, political scandals, environmental tragedies, toxic fumes, world starvation, the destruction of the ecosystem, landfills, an uprising epidemic of social anxiety, stress, and health issues with many people. Not to mention ongoing racism, trash island, scandalous oil drilling, electric cars which are absolutely not ethically made, natural disasters, homicide, suicide, and traumatic events that take place in people's lives that are hard to forget. Mental health crises are extremely valid along with the homeless population in America while third world countries struggle for basic necessities like food, water and shelter. Not to mention the bigotry, narcissism, racism, anti-woke vibes, anti-gender rights, and anti-feminism that takes place on earth. Let's just say we all have a lot of beach cleanups to do if you catch my drift (which is probably loaded with plastic by the way). However, there is progress that some people are aware of. Inventions like the home recycling and compost machines such as Lasso and Lomi could save the war on the landfills. There are people living next to landfills and surviving on selling anything they can find to survive. GreenPeace campaigns against worldwide problems such as climate change, deforestation, overfishing, and commercial whaling are helpful. NRDC- Natural Resources Defense Council is a non-profit environmental group founded in 1970 that has helped provide clean water, clean air, healthy communities, hold polluters accountable, protect animals, stand against corporations putting chemicals into our food, and participate in adopting clean energy solutions. There are companies that have made it accessible to get healthy food products, bath and body necessities, at home cleaning supplies, anything from upcycled furniture to items made out of recycled material- which are becoming more and more popular. Artists are creating material out of recycled material. Companies are practicing reusing and recycling and everyone is promoting a clean earth. Solutions are coming for sure, they are already here. Raise the vibration of your aura, your home, those around you, and the world- by taking the little steps and start thinking of ways to change this place. We are discovering a new way to practice human kindness and build community everyday. Have you ever heard of an Earthship? https://earthshipstore.com/collections/construction-drawings-offgrid

These are houses made out of all recycled material and green living. Galactic confederation FOREVER! Pleiadian vibes love yourself first! It will all come together naturally. We are one!! One big team we got this soul family! Hold your breath and dive deep into the sea of life! You can do it! *WE LOVE YOU ALL -THE GUIDES*

Divine Message

Reconstruction is necessary. We got this. We can handle this. We are meant to recreate and adapt to this beautiful natural environment. We are one. The world will know peace. This place will be a sanctuary for all living beings. *Everything* will be restored and forgiven. Rebuilt and transformed. The future is wonderful for everyone. *Just believe. You got this!* Have hope your destiny is calling you- follow that path!!! We are made up of the elements and stardust human beings are amazing and resilient !

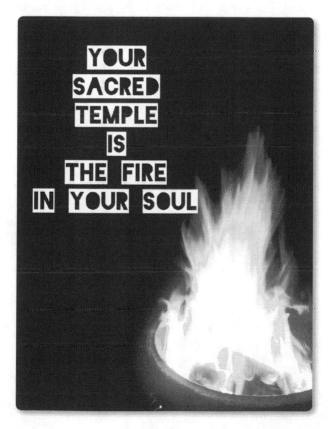

The Eye of Horus is an ancient Egyptian symbol of protection, Health, Restoration. Horus lost his left eye in a battle with Seth. It was magically restored by Heather making it whole and healed. The Eye of Horus protects from the evil eye and brings good luck.

What is known as "the evil eye" ◉ symbol, is actually associated with the Bavarian Illuminati secret society founded in 1776. This is a symbol of protection. Adam Weishaupt was a German philosopher who founded the secret society. Many people think it is associated with devil worship or fame and riches. It is actually a spiritual gateway to enlightenment. The collective consciousness will understand what it reveals one day. Illumination is protection. Religious propaganda will be exposed. All will be well.

Soul. Body. Enlightenment. Astral Travel. Reincarnation. Collective Spiritual Awakening.

Wherever you are on your path/journey in life, try to find <u>one way</u> to release negativity on a daily basis. I will tell you now a few ways to stay enlightened and "clear" or "vanish", "abduct", if you will, any negative debris/energy from where you are now to where you sleep each night or your energetic space. What I have learned is if you stay in "the self" too long, you may just become one with your ego. It is not so bad to be "shell-fish", but remember to stay positive and encouraging, compassionate, and kind.

What is one thing you have done for yourself today?

_____

_____

How have you helped another person this week?

_____

_____

A 12 year old did a backflip in the Starbucks that I am writing in; with the superpowers from hot chocolate. Thank you *Starbucks* for letting me write my book in peace and for the nice music. BE NICE TO YOUR BARISTA!!!! :)

Shout out to the Unitarian church in Fresno. Harmony and peace will happen!!! Best believe it!!! Universal equality and acceptance !!!

<3

Try more self help options because YOLO!!!

Cryotherapy
Oxygen Bar
Float Spas
Salt Caves
Hot Springs
Acro Yoga
Pole Dancing
Ecstatic Dance
Tantric/Kundalini Yoga

Vitamin Shots
Getting Massages
Exercise
Sobriety (lol)
Get involved with Community/Volunteer
Eat Healthy
Detoxing/Juicing
Stuff your face with vitamins
Saunas/Steam rooms
Beauty Regimens/Holistic Healing
Acupressure/Acupuncture
Tai Chi
Chi Gong
Reading Books/Researching
Getting your Protein in/more reps lol
Loving yourself unconditionally
Body positivity
Writing down your dreams
Call in your guides
Ask for help
Be patient
Remember divine timing
Your destiny is calling you
Write down your dreams
Find out what you love to do, *do that*

LOVE ALWAYS

KAT

It's really fun how we get to practice self love over and over
again. That should be a religion in itself. But anyways here

we are, doing it again. We are angels, saints, gods, and goddesses on earth reincarnated. It's about time to start treating each other as equals and recognizing the heart and mind in everything. Honesty, trust and using your intuitive nature is everything!! SO many things need to change for us to live in a harmonious way, and should change for the planet. We can find personal growth on a spiritual journey and trust-fall into the ocean of the universe and let the waves surround you. Things do happen for a reason (for you). Whether you believe in karma, fate, or destiny, the law of attraction and power of manifestation might help us save our own lives. Attracting, creating, harmonizing with each other. Have you ever thought, wow I am picking up that I should really do this, instead of what everyone is telling me to do, or you have that gut feeling to just give someone a hug. When you listen to the voices of the angels/daemon guides, we come closer in spirit to learning our lessons in life, so the universal power of one divine energy, can come up with more shit for us to learn about. MORE LIFE LESSONS! The Universe is testing us to see if we truly learn kindness and master ourselves. Karmic law is along the way. It's frustrating when things happen multiple times, believe me I know. The trick is to change the limiting beliefs, into positivity to reprogram your brain. The angels/demons/guides/universe will guide you into a new direction where another teaching is being held, uniquely, just for you. Then we can share our knowledge with each other. If you believe in yourself, continue to make unique choices and have safe travels on your Journey. Blessed be, xoxoxoxo, Kat

LIL MAMA GO
SPREAD YOUR WINGS-
RADICAL SOMETHING

my most favorite songs/bands ever..

She Talks to Angels by *The Black Crowes*
Dreams by *Fleetwood Mac*
She's My Religion by *Pale Waves*
Drops of Jupiter and Meet Virginia by *Train*
Blue- (The Thirteenth Step album)by *A Perfect Circle*
Burning Bright by *Shinedown*
She's so High by *Tal Bachman*

B*tch by *Meredith Brooks*
Sensitive *by Dreamer Isioma*
Best Thing *by Inayah*
Gin and Juice by *Snoop Dog*
Coming Home by *City and Colour*
Labour *by Paris Paloma*
Tell me all your thoughts on God by *The Stoesz*
The Way by *Mac Miller and Ariana Grande*
The Highway Song by *Kat Hasty*
opal ocean by *slenderbodies*
Zanzibar by *Kamaliza*
Serotonin *by girl in red*
Art Hoe by *Call Me Karizma*
Sex With Me by *TRAMP STAMPS*
H.O.E by *Speed Gang*
My Silver Lining by *First Aid Kit*
Poison and Wine *by The Civil Wars*
Jezebel by *Iron and Wine*
Skinny Love *by Bon Iver*
Not ur friend- *Jeremy Zucker*
Prayed for you- *Matt Stell*
GO 2 HELL and DRUGS by lil aaron
Mind Reader- *Dustin Lynch*
Love Her Too (*feat G-Eazy) and Marc E. Bassy*
You got it- *Vedo*
Cry Dancing- *NOTD and Nina Nesbitt*
Head & Heart (feat. MNEK)- *Joel Corry*
Dance Monkey by *Tones and I*
My Prerogative- by *Bobby Brown*
Burn Your Village by Kiki Rockwell
Don't F*cking Touch Me by Banshee

Bands: Odesza, Florence and the Machine, BANKS

Flume, Skrillex, Jaya Lakshmi and Ananda,Lund, Yemanjo, Hippie Sabotage, Tove Lo, MC YOGI, Gregorian, Iggy Azalea, Ashnikko,Whethan, Grandson, Sam Smith, Big Wild, Eminem and D12, Stone Sour, Petit Biscuit, The Chainsmokers,Arctic Monkeys, Zara Larsson, Russ, Jack Johnson, Tash Sultana, Pia Mia, Billie Ellish, KALEO, Bebe Rexha, ILLENIUM, X Ambassadors, Seether, Speed Gang, Willow, Koven, mansionz, blackbear, Rebelution, Tribal Seeds, Mabel, Matt Maeson, Delilah Bon, X Ambassadors, Hozier, Nova Twins, Doja Cat.

Let No Man Steal Your Thyme by *Pentangle*

May the Lightness and Darkness guide your path wherever you roam this earth. Ascension is possible for everyone!!! Find enlightenment, find yourself!! Listen to the voice within. Stay on that high vibration!!! Be yourself! Stay centered and focused and make those damn dreams come true!!! Do what you are passionate about !! And f*cking DANCE ALL NIGHT AT THE CLUB!!!! Kundalini movement is the new gateway to ASCENSION!!!

LOVE AND LIGHT

PEACE AND NAMASTE

WITH LOVE,

Kat

<3

Rock on!!! Xoxo

MAKE TODAY THE BEST DAY!!!!
I LOVE YOU!!!

CITED INFO

https://labs.theguardian.com/unicef-child-labour/

https://www.merriam-webster.com/words-at-play/asmr-abbreviation-meaning

https://www.oprahdaily.com/life/a29775503/palo-santo-benefits/

https://rsc.byu.edu/deity-death/comparative-study-ascension-motifs-world-religions
https://www.dictionary.com/browse/ascension

https://www.verywellhealth.com/mugwort-benefits-side-effects-dosage-and-interactions-47672266/Bej.9789004163737.i-650_004.xml

https://www.learnreligions.com/so-mote-it-be-2561921

https://cailleachs-herbarium.com/2019/02/saining-not-smudging-purification-and-lustration-in-scottish-folk-magic-practice/

https://en.wikipedia.org/wiki/Pentagram\

https://eragem.com/news/turquoise-meaning-symbolism/#:~:text=Turquoise%2C%20the%20captivating%20sea%2Dgreen,its%20association%20with%20enduring%20love.

https://www.charmsoflight.com/jade-healing-properties#:~:text=Jade%20is%20a%20symbol%20of,attracts%20good%20luck%20and%20friendship.

https://en.wikipedia.org/wiki/Kali

https://thehabitat.com/life/the-spiritual-meaning-of-angel-number-111/

https://cdn.shopify.com/s/files/1/0273/4214/3566/files/TinyRituals-Healing_Crystals_Guide.pdf?v=1633562407

https://symbolismandmetaphor.com/symbolism-of-earth/

https://www.universetoday.com/35931/symbols-of-the-planets/

https://www.shenyunperformingarts.org/explore/view/article/e/0waI6QyYWJM/bodhisattva-guan-yin.html

https://www.mindbodygreen.com/articles/the-4-types-of-intuition-and-how-to-tap-into-each

https://www.merriam-webster.com/dictionary/clairvoyant---

tazachocolate.com.

https://thehabitat.com/life/what-is-the-divine-meaning-of-angel-number-222/

https://thehabitat.com/life/what-does-angel-number-555-mean/

https://www.mindbodygreen.com/articles/vedic-astrology-101

https://thehabitat.com/life/angel-number-444-what-is-it-telling-you/

https://www.healthline.com/nutrition/foods/olives
https://www.healthline.com/nutrition/are-cashews-good-for-you
https://www.healthline.com/nutrition/avocados-and-weight#TOC TITLE HDR 4
https://www.mayoclinichealthsystem.org/hometown-health/speaking-of-health/the-many-types-and-health-benefits-of-kale#:~:text=NUTRITIONAL%20BENEFITS,friendly%2Fweight%2Dfriendly%20vegetable.

https://brill.com/view/book/edcoll/978904744235

https://www.greatlakespsychologygroup.com/blog/5-stages-grief/

https://thehabitat.com/life/why-you-keep-seeing-angel-number-888-everywhere/

https://thehabitat.com/life/is-seeing-angel-number-666-a-bad-sign/

https://thehabitat.com/life/angel-number-333-unlocking-your-message-from-the-universe/

https://boomboomnaturals.com/blogs/news/essential-oils-for-grief

https://www.myrecipes.com/news/can-you-get-drunk-from-kombucha#:~:text=You'd%20have%20to%20drink,effects%20similar%20to%20one%20beer.

https://thehabitat.com/life/the-significance-of-angel-number-777/

https://www.fluke.com/en-us/learn/blog/electrical/what-is-frequency#:~:text=Frequency%20is%20the%20rate%20at,to%20one%20cycle%20per%20second.

(https://www.youtube.com/watch?v=1yaqUI4b974)

https://www.rottentomatoes.com/m/500_days_of_summer/quotes/

https://en.wikipedia.org/wiki/Self-love

https://link.springer.com/article/10.1023/a:1018413522959

https://outside.vermont.gov/agency/agriculture/vpac/Shared%20Documents/January_2014/pathak_human_effects_10%205923%20j%20ije%2020110101%2003%20(2).pdf

https://guayaki.com/

https://healthiersteps.com/the-health-benefits-of-spring-water/

"The Angel Bible"- by Hazel Raven
And InnerLT. Resources, Inc : Rainbow Cards

Backyard Medicine by Julie Bruton-Seal & Matthew Seal

the online crystal guide -tinyrituals.co

http://www.mamuse.org/lyrics-heart-nouveau

https://moon.nasa.gov/resources/444/tides/#:~:text=The%20Moon%20and%20Earth%20exert,are%20where%20low%20tides%20occur.
https://a-z-animals.com/blog/coyote-spirit-animal-symbolism-meaning/

https://www.spiritanimal.info/wolf-spirit-animal/

https://www.thecollector.com/echo-narcissus-myth/

Printed in the United States
by Baker & Taylor Publisher Services